Nursery Treasury

Nursery Treasury

Miles Kelly
PUBLISHING

www.mileskelly.net

Copyright © Miles Kelly Publishing Ltd 2007

First published in 2007 by Miles Kelly Publishing Ltd
Bardfield Centre, Great Bardfield, Essex, CM7 4SL

Some of this material also appears in *50 Great Bedtime Stories*,
100 Best-Loved Nursery Rhymes.

2 4 6 8 10 9 7 5 3 1

Editorial Director Belinda Gallagher
Art Director Jo Brewer
Designer Candice Bekir
Cover Designer Jo Brewer
Reprographics Liberty Newton, Ian Paulyn
Production Manager Elizabeth Brunwin

British Library Cataloguing-in-Publication Data
A catalogue record for this book is available from the British Library

ISBN 978-1-84236-866-4

www.mileskelly.net
info@mileskelly.net

Contents

Girls and Boys

Favourite Folk

Best-Loved 358–445

Play Together

Round and Round the Garden

Round and round the garden

Like a teddy bear;

One step, two step,

Tickle you under there!

Draw circles with
your finger around
the palm.

Walk your fingers up
the arm in two steps.

Tickle under the arm!

Here is the Church

Here is the church, and here is the steeple;

Open the door and here are the people.

Here is the parson going upstairs,

And here he is a-saying his prayers.

Put palms together and link fingers downwards to form the church.

Point index fingers up to form the spire.

Turn hands over and wiggle the fingers to be the people.

This Little Pig

This little pig went to market,

This little pig stayed at home,

This little pig had roast beef,

This little pig had none,

Read the first line and wiggle the big toe.

Read the next line and wiggle the next toe and so on...

On the final line tickle the foot.

And this little pig cried,

"Wee-wee-wee-wee-wee!"

All the way home.

The Three Little Pigs

An English folk tale

There once was a mother pig who had three little pigs. They were very poor indeed, and the day came when the mother pig could no longer look after the family. She sent the three little pigs out into the big, wide world to seek their fortunes.

The first little pig met a man carrying a big bundle of straw.

"Oh, please may I have that bundle of straw to build myself a house?" asked the first little pig. The man was tired of carrying the bundle of straw so he gladly gave it to the first little pig.

The first little pig built a very fine house out of the bundle of straw, and he lived there very happily. Then along came a big bad wolf.

"Little pig, little pig, let me come in!" shouted the wolf.

"No, no, not by the hair on my chinny chin chin. I'll not let you in," squeaked the first little pig.

"Then I'll huff and I'll puff, and I'll blow your house down," yelled the wolf. And he did. He huffed and he puffed and he blew the straw house down. The first little pig ran away as fast as his trotters would carry him.

Now the second little pig met a man carrying a bundle of sticks.

"Oh, please may I have that bundle of sticks to build myself a house?" asked the second little pig. The man was tired of carrying the bundle of sticks so he gladly gave it to the second little pig.

The second little pig built a very fine house out of the sticks, and he lived there very happily.

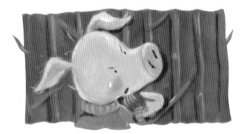

Then along came the big bad wolf.

"Little pig, little pig, let me come in!" shouted the wolf.

"No, no, not by the hair on my chinny chin chin. I'll not let you in," squeaked the second little pig.

"Then I'll huff and I'll puff, and I'll blow your house down," yelled the wolf. And he did. He huffed and he puffed and he blew the stick house down. The second little pig ran away as fast as his trotters would carry him.

Now the third little pig met a man carrying a big load of bricks.

"Oh, please may I have that load of bricks to build myself a house?" asked the third little pig. The man was very tired from carrying the big load of bricks so he gave it to the third little pig.

The third little pig built a very fine house out of the bricks, and he lived there very happily. Then along came the big bad wolf.

"Little pig, little pig, let me come in!" shouted the wolf.

"No, no, not by the hair on my chinny chin chin. I'll not let you in," squeaked the third little pig.

"Then I'll huff and I'll puff, and I'll blow your house down," yelled the wolf. And he tried. He huffed and he puffed but he could not blow the brick house down.

"Little pig, little pig, I am coming down your chimney to get you," bellowed the wolf.

"Please yourself," called the third little pig who was busy with some preparations of his own.

"Little pig, little pig, I have my front paws down your chimney," threatened the wolf.

"Please yourself," called the third little pig who was still busy with some preparations of his own.

"Little pig, little pig, I have my great bushy tail down your chimney," called the wolf.

"Please yourself," called the third little pig who was now sitting in his rocking chair by the fireside.

"Little pig, little pig, here I come!" and with a great rush and a huge SPLOSH! the big bad wolf fell right into the big pot of boiling water that the clever little pig had placed on the fire,

right under the chimney. The wolf scrabbled and
splashed and scrambled out of the big pot and
ran as fast as ever he could right out of the front
door. And he was never seen again. The third
little pig managed to find his two brothers, and
they went and fetched their mother. And they
are all still living happily together in the little
brick house.

Pat-a-Cake

Pat-a-cake, pat-a-cake, baker's man,

Bake me a cake as fast as you can;

Roll it and pat it and mark it with 'B',

And put it in the oven for baby and me.

Clap your hands together then pat the palms of your partner.

Repeat this action as you sing the rhyme.

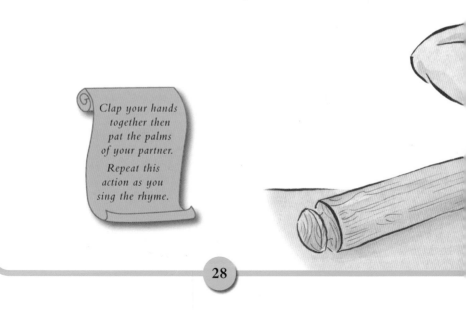

If you're Happy and you Know it

If you're happy and you know it,

clap your hands.

If you're happy and you know it,

clap your hands.

If you're happy and you know it

and you really want to show it,

If you're happy and you know it

clap your hands.

Repeat the words again, but change the action to stamping your feet, clicking your fingers and touching your head.

Oranges and Lemons

Oranges and lemons,

Say the bells of St. Clement's.

You owe me five farthings,

Say the bells of St. Martin's.

When will you pay me?

Say the bells of

Old Bailey.

Two children
representing oranges and
lemons form an arch.

The other children
pass beneath.

On the final verse, the
arch falls and the
child beneath chooses
to stand behind
'oranges' or 'lemons'.

When I grow rich,
Say the bells of Shoreditch.

When will that be?
Say the bells of Stepney.

I do not know,
Says the great bell of Bow.

Here comes a candle
To light you to bed.

Here comes
a chopper
To chop off
your head!

Ring-a-ring o' Roses

Ring-a-ring o' roses,

A pocket full of posies,

A-tishoo! A-tishoo!

We all fall down.

*All hold hands and
skip round in a ring.*

*On the last line
of each verse, all sit
down on the ground.*

See-saw, Margery Daw

See-saw, Margery Daw,

Johnny shall have a new master;

He shall have but a penny a day,

Because he can't work any faster.

An ideal rhyme for playing in the park.

Or sit on the floor facing your partner holding hands.

Gently rock backwards and forwards as if you were on a see-saw.

37

Two Little Dickie-birds

Two little dickie-birds,

Sitting on a wall,

One named Peter,

The other named Paul.

Fly away, Peter!

Fly away, Paul!

Come back, Peter!

Come back, Paul!

Use your index fingers to be Peter and Paul.

Wiggle each finger in turn.

Next, put each finger behind you as if to fly away.

On the last line, bring each finger back in front of you.

I'm a Little Teapot

I'm a little teapot,

Short and stout,

Here's my handle,

Here's my spout.

When I see the teacups,

Hear me shout,

"Tip me up, and pour me out!"

Place one hand on your hip to be the handle.

Place the opposite arm out to the side to be the spout.

On the final line, lean over to the side to pour the tea.

The Mulberry Bush

Here we go round the mulberry bush,

The mulberry bush, the mulberry bush,

Here we go round the mulberry bush,

On a cold and frosty morning.

This is the way we wash our hands,

Wash our hands, wash our hands,

This is the way we wash our hands,

On a cold and frosty morning.

This is the way we wash our clothes,

Wash our clothes, wash our clothes,

This is the way we wash our clothes,

On a cold and frosty morning.

Join hands and skip round in a circle on the first verse.

This is the chorus.

Mime the actions in the remaining verses.

After each main verse repeat the chorus.

This is the way we go to school,

Go to school, go to school,

This is the way we go to school,

On a cold and frosty morning.

This is the way we come out of school,

Come out of school, come out of school,

This is the way we come out of school,

On a cold and frosty morning.

Head, Shoulders, Knees and Toes

Head, shoulders, knees and toes,

Knees and toes,

Head, shoulders, knees and toes,

Knees and toes,

And eyes and ears and mouth and nose,

Head, shoulders, knees and toes,

Knees and toes.

Touch each part of the body as you sing the rhyme.

This is the Way

This is the way the ladies ride,

Tri, tre, tre, tree, Tri, tre, tre, tree;

This is the way the ladies ride,

Tri, tre, tre, tre, tri-tre-tre-tree!

Pretend to be a lady gently riding along. Next pretend to be a gentleman galloping along. Then pretend to be a farmer hobbling along.

This is the way the gentlemen ride,

Gallop-a-trip, Gallop-a-trot;

This is the way the gentlemen ride,

Gallop-a-gallop-a-trot!

This is the way the farmers ride,

Hobbledy-hoy, Hobbledy-hoy;

This is the way the farmers ride,

Hobbledy, hobbledy-hoy!

Row, Row, Row your Boat

Row, row, row your boat,

Gently down the stream.

Merrily, merrily, merrily, merrily,

Life is but a dream.

Singers sit
opposite one
another and 'row'
forwards and
backwards with
joined hands.

One Potato

One potato, two potatoes,

Three potatoes, four,

Five potatoes, six potatoes,

Seven potatoes more.

Take turns with your partner in placing one fist on top of another to build a tower. When you reach seven start again.

The Magic Porridge Pot

A Swedish folk tale

One day, just before Christmas, a poor old farmer and his wife decided that they needed to sell their last cow. They had no money left and no food in the cupboard. As the farmer walked sadly to market with the cow, he met a very strange little man on the way. He had a long white beard right down to his toes, which were bare, and he wore a huge black hat, under which the farmer could only just see the bright gleam of his eyes. Over his arm he carried a battered old porridge pot.

"That's a nice looking cow," said the little man. "Is she for sale?"

"Yes," said the farmer.

"I shall buy your cow," declared the little man, putting the porridge pot down with a thump. "I shall give you this porridge pot in exchange for your cow!"

Well, the farmer looked at the battered old porridge pot, and he looked at his fine cow. And he was just about to say, "Certainly not!" when a voice whispered, "Take me! Take me!"

The farmer shook himself. Dear me, it was bad enough to be poor without beginning to hear strange voices. He opened his mouth again to say, "Certainly not!" when he heard the voice again. "Take me! Take me!"

Well, he saw at once that it must be a magic pot, and he knew you didn't hang about with magic pots, so he said very quickly to the little man, "Certainly!" and handed over the cow. He bent down to pick up the pot, and when he looked up, the little man had vanished.

The farmer knew he was going to have a difficult time explaining to his wife just how he had come to part with their precious cow for a battered old porridge pot.

She was very angry indeed and had started to say a lot of very cross things when a voice came from the pot,

"Take me inside and clean me and polish me, and you shall see what you shall see!"

Well, the farmer's wife was astonished but she did as she was bid. She washed the pot inside and out, and then she polished it until it shone as bright as a new pin. No sooner had she finished

than the pot hopped off the table, and out of the
door. The farmer and his wife sat down by the
fire, not saying a word to each other. They had
no money, no cow, no food and now it seemed
they didn't even have their magic pot.

Down the road from the poor farmer, there
lived a rich man. He was a selfish man who
spent all his time eating huge meals and
counting his money. He had lots of servants,
including a cook who was in the kitchen
making a Christmas pudding. The pudding was
stuffed with plums, currants, sultanas, almonds
and goodness knows what else. It
was so big that the cook
realized she didn't have a
pot to boil it in. It was at
this point that the
porridge pot trotted in
the door.

"Goodness me!" she exclaimed. "The fairies must have sent this pot just in time to take my pudding," and she dropped the pudding in the pot. No sooner had the pudding fallen to the bottom with a very satisfying thud, than the pot skipped out of the door again. The cook gave a great shriek, but by the time the butler and the footman and the parlour maid and the boy who turned the spit had all dashed into the kitchen, the pot was quite out of sight.

The porridge pot in the meantime trotted down the road to the poor farmer's house. He and his wife were delighted to see the pot again, and even more pleased when they discovered the wonderful pudding. The wife boiled it up and it lasted them for three days. So they had a good Christmas after all, while the old porridge pot sat quietly by the fire.

Spring came, and still the porridge pot sat quietly by the fire. Then one day the pot suddenly trotted over to the farmer's wife and said, "Clean me, and polish me, and you shall see what you shall see."

So the farmer's wife polished the pot till it shone as bright as a new pin.

No sooner had she finished than the pot hopped off the table, and out of the door.

You will remember that the rich man was very fond of counting his money. There he sat in the great hall, with piles of golden guineas and silver sixpences on the table, and great bulging bags of coins on the floor at his feet. He was wondering where he could hide the money when in trotted the pot. Now the cook had been far too frightened of the rich man's temper to tell him about the pot stealing the Christmas pudding, so when he saw the pot he was delighted.

"Goodness me!" he exclaimed, "The fairies must have sent this pot just in time to take my money," and he dropped several bags of money in the pot. No sooner had the bags fallen to the bottom with a very satisfying clink, than the pot skipped out of the door again. The rich man shouted and hollered, but by the time the coachman and the head groom and the stable lad had run into the great hall, the pot was quite out of sight.

It trotted down the road to the poor farmer's house. He and his wife were delighted to see the pot again, and even more pleased when they discovered the bags of gold and silver. There was enough money to last them for the rest of their days, even after they had bought a new cow.

As for the battered old porridge pot, it sat by the fire for many a long year. Then, one day, it

suddenly trotted straight out of the door. It went
off up the road until it was out of sight, and the
farmer and his wife never saw it again.

Incy Wincy Spider

Incy Wincy Spider
Climbed up the water spout;
Down came the rain
And washed the spider out:

Use your fingers to be the spider climbing up the spout.

Wriggle your fingers to be the rain.

Sweep your hands in an arch to show the sun.

Use your fingers to be the spider climbing back up the spout.

Out came the sun
And dried up all the rain;
So Incy Wincy Spider
Climbed up the spout again.

The Wheels on the Bus

The wheels on the bus

go round and round,

Round and round, round and round.

The wheels on the bus

go round and round,

All day long.

(Roll your hands over each other)

The horn on the bus goes,
"Beep, beep, beep! Beep, beep, beep!
Beep, beep, beep!"
The horn on the bus goes,
"Beep, beep, beep!"
All day long.

(Pretend to honk the horn)

The windscreen wipers go, "Swish, swish, swish!

Swish, swish, swish! Swish, swish, swish!"

The windscreen wipers go,

"Swish, swish, swish!"

All day long.

(Swish your arms like windscreen wipers)

The people on the bus bounce up and down,

Up and down, up and down.

The people on the bus

bounce up and down,

All day long.

(Bounce up and down)

The daddies on the bus go nod, nod nod,

Nod, nod, nod, nod, nod, nod.

The daddies on the bus go nod, nod, nod,

All day long.

(Nod your head)

The mummies on the bus go

Chatter, chatter, chatter,

Chatter, chatter, chatter,

Chatter, chatter, chatter.

The mummies on the bus go

Chatter, chatter, chatter,

All day long.

(Open and close your fingers and thumb)

Animal Friends

Ding, Dong Bell

Ding, dong bell,

Pussy's in the well.

Who put her in?

Little Johnny Green.

Who pulled her out?

Little Johnny Stout.

What a naughty boy was that

To try to drown poor pussy cat,

Who never did him any harm,

But killed the mice in his father's barn.

Pussy Cat, Pussy Cat

Pussy cat, pussy cat, where have you been?

I've been to London to look at the queen.

Pussy cat, pussy cat, what did you there?

I frightened a little mouse under her chair.

A Cat came Fiddling

A cat came fiddling out of a barn,

With a pair of bagpipes under her arm.

She could sing nothing but fiddle dee dee,

The mouse has married the bumblebee.

Pipe, cat; dance, mouse;

We'll have a wedding

at our good house.

The Ugly Duckling

A retelling from the original story by Hans Christian Anderson

The mother duck was waiting for her eggs to hatch. Slowly the first shell cracked and first a tiny bill and then a little yellow wing appeared. Then with a great rush, a bedraggled yellow duckling fell out. He stretched his wings and began to clean his feathers. Soon he stood proudly beside his mother, watching as his sisters and brothers all pushed their way out of their shells.

There was only one shell left. It was the largest, and the mother duck wondered why it was taking so much longer than the others. She wanted to take her babies down to the river for their first swimming lesson. There was a sudden

loud crack, and there lay quite the biggest
and ugliest duckling she had ever seen. He
wasn't even yellow. His feathers were dull brown
and grey.

"Oh dear," said the mother duck.

She led the family down to the river, the ugly
duckling trailing along behind the others. They
all splashed into the water, and were soon
swimming gracefully, all except the ugly
duckling who looked large and ungainly even
on the water.

"Oh dear," said the mother duck.

The whole family set off for the farmyard

where they were greeted with hoots and moos
and barks and snorts from all the other animals.

"Whatever is that?" said the rooster, pointing
rudely at the ugly duckling. All the other
ducklings huddled round their mother and tried
to pretend the ugly duckling was not with them.

"Oh dear," said the mother duck.

The ugly duckling felt very sad and lonely.
No one seemed to like him, so he ran away from
the farmyard and hid in some dark reeds by the
river. Some hunters came by
with their loud noisy guns
and big fierce dogs. The
ugly duckling paddled
deeper into the reeds,
trembling with fear.
Only later in the day,
as it was growing
dark, did the ugly

duckling stir from his hiding place.

All summer he wandered over fields and down rivers. Everywhere he went people laughed and jeered at him, and all the other ducks he met just hissed at him or tried to bite his tail. As well as being ugly, the duckling was very lonely and unhappy. Soon winter came and the rivers began to freeze over. One day the duckling found himself trapped in the ice. He tucked his head under his wing, and decided that his short life must have come to an end.

He was still there early the next morning when a farmer came by on his way to feed the cows in the fields. The farmer broke the ice with his shoe, and wrapped the ugly duckling in his jacket then carried him home to his children. They put the poor frozen ugly duckling in a box by the fire, and as he thawed out they fed him and stroked his feathers. And there the ugly duckling stayed through the winter, growing bigger all the time.

Now the farmer's wife had never had much time for the ugly duckling. He was always getting under her feet in the kitchen, and he was so clumsy that he kept knocking things over. He spilt the milk in the bucket from the cow. He put his great feet in the freshly churned butter. He was just a nuisance, and one day the farmer's wife had enough. So, in a rage, she chased him out of her kitchen, out of the farmyard and through the gate down the lane.

It was a perfect spring day. The apple trees were covered in blossom, the grass was green and the air was filled with the sound of birdsong. The ugly duckling wandered down to the river, and there he saw three magnificent pure white swans. They were so beautiful and graceful as they glided over towards the bank where he stood.

He waited for them to hiss at him and beat the water with their wings to frighten him away, but they didn't do any such thing. Instead they called him to come and join them. At first he thought it was a joke, but they asked him again.

He bent down to get into the water, and there looking back at him was his own reflection. But where was the ugly duckling? All he could see was another great and magnificent swan. He was a swan! Not an ugly duckling, but a swan. He lifted his long elegant neck, and called in sheer delight, "I am a swan! I am a SWAN!"and he sailed gracefully over the water to join his real family.

Goosey, Goosey Gander

Goosey, goosey gander,

Whither shall I wander?

Upstairs and downstairs

And in my lady's chamber.

There I met an old man

Who would not say his prayers,

I took him by his left leg

And threw him down the stairs.

Ducks' Ditty

All along the backwater,

Through the rushes tall,

Ducks are a-dabbling.

Up tails all!

Ducks' tails, drakes' tails,

Yellow feet a-quiver,

Yellow bills all out of sight

Busy in the river!

Slushy green undergrowth

Where the roach swim

Here we keep our larder,

Cool and full and dim.

Every one for what he likes!

We like to be

Heads down, tails up,

Dabbling free!

High in the blue above

Swifts whirl and call

We are down a-dabbling

Up tails all!

Kenneth Grahame
1859–1932, b. Scotland

High in the Pine Tree

High in the pine tree,
The little turtledove
Made a little nursery
To please her little love.

"Coo," said the turtledove,
"Coo," said she,
In the long shady branches
Of the dark pine tree.

The Crocodile

If you should meet a crocodile

Don't take a stick and poke him.

Ignore the welcome in his smile,

Be careful not to stroke him.

For as he sleeps upon the Nile,

He thinner gets and thinner;

So whene'er you meet a crocodile

He's ready for his dinner.

Who Killed Cock Robin?

Who killed Cock Robin?
"I," said the sparrow,
"With my bow and arrow,
I killed Cock Robin."

Who saw him die?
"I," said the fly,
"With my little eye,
I saw him die."

Who caught his blood?
"I," said the fish,
"With my little dish,
I caught his blood."

Who'll dig his grave?
"I," aid the owl,
"With my spade and trowel,
I'll dig his grave."

Who'll be the clerk?
"I," said the lark,
"If it's not in the dark,
I'll be the clerk."

Who'll be the parson?
"I," said the rook,
"With my little book,
I'll be the parson."

Who'll sing a psalm?
"I," said the thrush,
As she sat on a bush,
"I'll sing a psalm."

Who'll be chief mourner?
"I," said the dove,
"I mourn for my love,
I'll be chief mourner."

Who'll toll the bell?
"I," said the bull,
"Because I can pull,
I'll toll the bell."

All the birds of the air
Fell sighing and sobbing,
When they heard the bell toll
For poor Cock Robin.

To all it concerns,
This notice apprises,
The sparrow's for trial
At the next bird assizes.

Pussy Cat Mole

Pussy Cat Mole
Jumped over a coal
And in her best petticoat
Burnt a great hole.

Poor pussy's weeping,
She'll have no more milk
Until her best petticoat's
Mended with silk.

Mary's Lamb

Mary had a little lamb,

Its fleece was white as snow;

And everywhere that Mary went

The lamb was sure to go.

It followed her to school one day,

That was against the rules.

It made the children laugh and play,

To see a lamb at school.

The Cow

The friendly cow all red and white,

I love with all my heart;

She gives me cream with all her might,

To eat with apple tart.

She wanders lowing here and there,

And yet she cannot stray,

All in the pleasant open air,

The pleasant light of day;

And blown by all the winds that pass

And wet with all the showers,

She walks among the meadow grass

And eats the meadow flowers.

Robert Louis Stevenson
1850–94, b. Scotland

The Lion and the Unicorn

The Lion and the Unicorn

Were fighting for the crown;

The Lion beat the Unicorn

All about the town.

Some gave them white bread

And some gave them brown;

Some gave them plum cake

And drummed them out of town!

Little Bo-peep

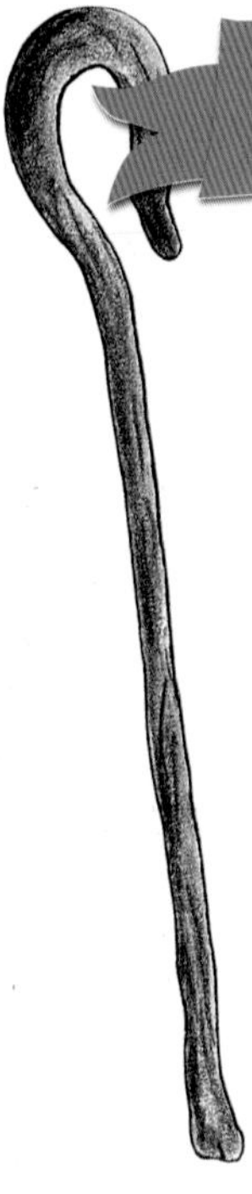

Little Bo-peep
has lost her sheep,
And can't tell where
to find them;
Leave them alone,
and they'll come home,
Bringing their tails
behind them.

Little Red Riding Hood

There was once a little girl who lived in the middle of a deep, dark forest with her mother and father, who was a woodcutter. The little girl always wore a red cloak with a hood, and so she was called Little Red Riding Hood.

One day she decided to visit her granny who lived some way from the woodcutter's cottage. She took a basket with a cake her mother had baked and set off. Now the last thing her mother had said to Little Red Riding Hood was, "Don't leave the path, and don't talk to any strangers." But Little Red Riding Hood was not really listening. So when she saw some bluebells growing under a tree, she left the path and began to pick a bunch for her granny. Slowly,

slowly she wandered further away from the path,
deeper into the trees. Suddenly, she was not
alone. There in front of her stood a great big
wolf. Now Little Red Riding Hood had not met

a wolf before so she did not realize that wolves are not the kind of animals to be too friendly with.

"Good day, little girl," said the wolf with a snarly sort of a smile. "What is your name and where are you going?"

"My name is Little Red Riding Hood. I am going to visit my granny, and I am taking her a cake to eat," replied Little Red Riding Hood.

The wolf was delighted. Not only a little girl to eat but a granny AND a cake as well!

"And where does your granny live, little girl?" asked the wolf, trying hard to smile nicely despite his fierce teeth.

Little Red Riding Hood told the wolf where her granny lived, and went on picking bluebells. The wolf slipped away through the trees and soon found the granny's cottage. He tapped on the door and said, in a disguised voice, "Hello, granny. It is Little Red Riding Hood. I have brought you a cake, will you let me in?"

As soon as the door was open, the wolf bounded in and gobbled the granny all up! He put on her nightcap and shawl and climbed into her bed. Soon he heard Little Red Riding Hood coming and he tried his snarly smile again.

"Hello, granny," said Little Red Riding Hood. "I have brought you a cake and these bluebells," and she came up to the bedside.

"Goodness, granny! What great big eyes you have!" she said.

"All the better to see you with," growled the wolf.

Little Red Riding Hood could not help noticing the wolf's teeth.

"Goodness, granny!

What great big teeth you have!"

"All the better to eat you with!" snapped the
wolf and gobbled Little Red Riding Hood up.

He gobbled up the cake in the basket as well and then, very full indeed, he fell fast asleep, snoring loudly.

Now by great good luck, Little Red Riding Hood's father was passing by the cottage, and when he heard the terrible snores he put his head round the door to see who was making such a noise. He was horrified to see the wolf so he took his axe and made a great slit down the wolf's tummy. Out jumped Little Red Riding Hood. Out staggered granny. She stitched up the wolf's tummy and told him to mind his manners in future. Then, as there was no cake left for tea, they all went back home, and Little Red Riding

Hood's mother made pancakes. I am pleased to
say Little Red Riding Hood had learnt her
lesson, and she never spoke to wolves again.

The Cat and the Fiddle

Hey-diddle-diddle,

The cat and the fiddle,

The cow jumped over the moon;

The little dog laughed to see such fun,

And the dish ran away with the spoon.

Hickory, Dickory, Dock

Hickory, dickory, dock,

The mouse ran up the clock.

The clock struck one,

The mouse ran down,

Hickory, dickory, dock.

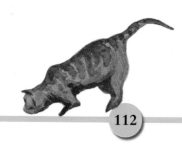

Hickety, Pickety

Hickety, pickety, my fine hen,
She lays eggs for gentlemen;
Gentlemen come every day
To see what my fine hen doth lay.
Sometimes nine and sometimes ten,
Hickety, pickety, my fine hen.

Where, O Where

Where, O where,

Has my little dog gone?

O where, O where, can he be?

With his tail cut short,

And his ears cut long,

O where, O where, has he gone?

Baa, Baa, Black Sheep

Baa, baa, black sheep,

Have you any wool?

Yes, sir, yes, sir,

Three bags full;

One for my master,

One for my dame,

And one for the little boy

Who lives down the lane.

I Love Little Pussy

I love little pussy, her coat is so warm,
And if I don't hurt her, she'll do me no harm.
So I'll not pull her tail, nor drive her away,
But pussy and I very gently will play.
I'll sit by the fire, and give her some food,
And pussy will love me because I am good.

To Market, to Market

To market, to market to buy a fat pig,

Home again, home again, jiggety-jig;

To market, to market to buy a fat hog,

Home again, home again, jiggety-jog.

Ride a Cock-horse

Ride a cock-horse to Banbury Cross,

To see a fine lady upon a white horse;

Rings on her fingers and bells on her toes,

She shall have music wherever she goes.

Cock a Doodle Doo

Cock a doodle doo!
My dame has lost her shoe;
My master's lost his
Fiddling stick
And doesn't know
what to do.

What does the Bee do?

What does the bee do?

What does the bee do?

Bring home honey.

And what does Father do?

Bring home money.

And what does Mother do?

Lay out the money.

And what does baby do?

Eat up the honey.

Christina Rossetti
1830–94, b. England

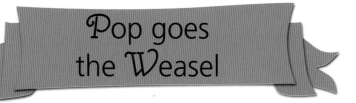

Pop goes the Weasel

Up and down the City Road,

In and out of the Eagle,

That's the way the money goes,

Pop goes the weasel!

Half a pound of tuppenny rice,

Half a pound of treacle,

Mix it up and make it nice,

Pop goes the weasel!

Every night when I go out

The monkey's on the table;

Take a stick and knock it off,

Pop goes the weasel.

Old Macdonald had a Farm

Old Macdonald had a farm,

E-I-E-I-O!

And on that farm he had some cows,

E-I-E-I-O!

With a moo-moo here,

And a moo-moo there,

Here a moo, there a moo,

everywhere a moo-moo,

Old Macdonald

had a farm,

E-I-E-I-O!

Old Macdonald had a farm,

E-I-E-I-O!

And on that farm he had some sheep,

E-I-E-I-O!

With a baa-baa here,

And a baa-baa there,

Here a baa, there a baa,

everywhere a baa-baa,

Old Macdonald

had a farm,

E-I-E-I-O!

Old Macdonald had a farm,

E-I-E-I-O!

And on that farm he had some ducks,

E-I-E-I-O!

With a quack-quack here,

And a quack-quack there,

Here a quack, there a quack,

everywhere a quack-quack,

Old Macdonald

had a farm,

E-I-E-I-O!

Old Macdonald had a farm,

E-I-E-I-O!

And on that farm he had some pigs,

E-I-E-I-O!

With an oink-oink here,

And an oink-oink there,

Here an oink, there an oink,

everywhere an oink-oink,

Old Macdonald

had a farm,

E-I-E-I-O!

Girls and Boys

Jack and Jill

Jack and Jill went up the hill

To fetch a pail of water;

Jack fell down, and broke his crown,

And Jill came tumbling after.

Then up Jack got, and home did trot,

As fast as he could caper.

He went to bed,

To mend his head

With vinegar and brown paper.

Jack and the Beanstalk

A retelling from the original tale by Joseph Jacobs

This is the story of how Jack did a silly thing, but all was well in the end.

Jack and his mother were very poor and there came a sad day when there was no more money left, so Jack was told to take the cow to market to sell her.

As Jack led the cow to market, he met a

funny little man with a tall feather in his hat.

"And where might you be going with that fine-looking cow?" the funny little man asked.

Jack explained and the little man swept off his hat with the tall feather, and shook out five coloured beans.

"Well, young Jack, I can save you a journey. I will give you these five magic beans in exchange for your cow."

Now Jack should have realized that this was all rather odd, for how did the funny little man know his name? But once he heard the word 'magic' he didn't stop to think.

He took the beans at once, gave the funny little man the cow and ran off home to his mother.

"Jack, you are a complete fool! You have exchanged our fine cow for five worthless beans!" She flung the beans out of the window, and sent Jack to bed without any supper.

When he woke in the morning, Jack couldn't understand why it was so dark in the cottage. He rushed outside to find his mother staring in amazement at the most enormous beanstalk that reached right up into the clouds.

"I told you they were magic beans," smiled Jack, and without any hesitation he began to climb the beanstalk. He climbed and climbed until he could no longer see the ground below. When he reached the top there stood a vast castle. Jack knocked at the door, and it was opened by a HUGE woman!

"My husband eats little boys for breakfast so

you better run away quickly," she said to Jack.
But before Jack could reply, the ground started
to shake and tremble.

"Too late!" said the giant's wife.
"You must hide,"
and she bundled Jack into
a cupboard. Jack
peeped through the
keyhole, and saw the
most colossal man.
"Fee fi fo fum! I
smell the blood of
an Englishman!"
he roared.

"Don't be
silly, dear. You
can smell the
sausages I
have just

cooked for your breakfast," said the giant's wife, placing a plate piled high with fat, juicy sausages in front of him. The giant did not seem to have very good table manners, and had soon gobbled the lot. Then he poured a great bag of gold onto the table, and counted all the coins. With a smile on his big face, he soon fell asleep.

Jack darted out of the cupboard, grabbed the bag of money and ran out of the kitchen. He slithered down the beanstalk as fast as he could and there, standing at the bottom, was his mother. She was amazed when she saw the gold.

Jack's mother bought two new cows and she and Jack were very content now they had plenty to eat. But after a while Jack decided he would like to climb the beanstalk again. The giant's wife was not very pleased to see him.

"My husband lost a bag of gold the last time you were here," she muttered looking closely at Jack, but then the ground began to shake and tremble. Jack hid in the cupboard again.

The giant stomped into the kitchen.

"Fee fi fo fum! I smell the blood of an Englishman!" he roared.

"Don't be silly, dear. You can smell the chickens I have just cooked for your breakfast," said the giant's wife, placing a plate piled high with thirty-eight chickens in front of him. The giant had soon gobbled the lot. Then he lifted a golden hen onto the table, and said, "Lay!" and the hen laid a golden egg. With a smile on his big face he fell asleep, snoring loudly.

Jack darted out of the cupboard, grabbed the golden hen and ran out of the kitchen. He slithered down the beanstalk as fast as ever he could and there, still standing at the bottom, was his mother. She was astonished when she saw the hen.

Jack's mother bought a whole herd of cows and found a farmer to look after them. She bought lots of new clothes for herself and Jack, and they were very content. But after a while Jack decided he would like to climb the beanstalk one last time. The giant's wife was not pleased to see him.

"My husband lost a golden hen the last time you were here," and she peered closely at Jack, but then the ground began to shake and tremble.

This time Jack hid under the table.

The giant stomped into the kitchen.

"Fee fi fo fum! I smell the blood of an Englishman!" he roared.

"I would look in the cupboard if I were you," said the giant's wife, but of course the cupboard was empty. They were both puzzled. The giant trusted his nose, and his wife didn't know where Jack had gone.

"Eat your breakfast, dear. I have just cooked you ninety-two fried eggs," said the giant's wife, placing a plate in front of him. The giant had soon gobbled the lot. Then he lifted a golden harp onto the table, and said, "Play!" and the harp played so sweetly that the giant was soon fast asleep, snoring loudly.

Jack crept out from under the table and grabbed the golden harp, but as soon as he touched it the harp called out, "Master, master!" and the giant awoke with a great start. He chased after Jack who scrambled down the beanstalk as fast as he could with the harp in his arms. As soon as Jack reached the ground he raced to get a big axe and chopped through the beanstalk. Down tumbled the great beanstalk, down tumbled the giant and that was the end of them both!

Jack and his mother lived very happily for the rest of their days. The bag of gold never ran out, the hen laid a golden egg every day, and the harp soon forgot about the giant and played sweetly for Jack and his mother.

Jack Sprat

Jack Sprat could eat no fat,

His wife could eat no lean,

So between them both, you see,

They licked the platter clean.

Jack ate all the lean,

Joan ate all the fat,

The bone they picked it clean,

Then gave it to the cat.

There was an Old Man

There was an Old Man

with a beard,

Who said,

"It is just as I feared!

Two owls and a hen,

Four larks and a wren,

Have all built their nests

in my beard!'

Edward Lear
1812–88, b. England

148

Georgie Porgie

Georgie Porgie, pudding and pie,

Kissed the girls and made them cry;

When the boys came out to play,

Georgie Porgie ran away.

Girls and Boys

Girls and boys, come out to play,

The moon is shining bright as day;

Leave your supper and leave your sleep,

And come with your playfellows into the street;

Come with a whoop and come with a call,

Come with a good will, or come not at all.

There was a Little Girl

There was a little girl and she had a little curl

Right in the middle of her forehead;

When she was good, she was very, very good,

But when she was bad, she was horrid.

Rapunzel

A retelling from the original fairytale by the Brothers Grimm

Once upon a time there lived a man and his wife who for years and years had wanted a child. One day the wife was looking sadly out of the window. Winter was coming but in the next door garden, which was surrounded by a huge great wall, she could just see rows and rows of delicious-looking vegetables. In particular, she could see a huge bunch of rapunzel, a special kind of lettuce. Her mouth watered, it looked so fresh and green.

"Husband, I shall not rest until I have some of

that rapunzel growing next door," she whispered. The husband clambered over the wall and quickly picked a small bunch which he took back to his wife. She made it into a salad, and ate it all up. But the next day, all she could think of was how delicious it had been so she asked him to pick her some more.

He clambered over the wall, and was picking a small bunch of the rapunzel when a voice behind him hissed, "So you are the one who has been stealing my rapunzel!"

When he spun round, there stood a witch and she looked very angry indeed. The husband was terrified, but he tried to explain that his wife had been desperate for fresh leaves for her salad.

"You may take all the leaves you require then, but you must give me your first child when she is born," smiled the witch, and it was not a nice smile. The husband was greatly relieved, however, for he knew that there was little chance of his wife ever having a daughter so he fled back over the wall, clutching the bunch of rapunzel. He did not tell his wife of his meeting with the witch for he thought it would only frighten her, and he soon forgot all about his adventure.

But it all came back to him when nine months later his wife gave birth to a beautiful baby girl. No sooner had she laid the baby in her cradle, than the witch appeared to claim the child. The

wife wept, the husband pleaded but nothing
could persuade the witch to forget the husband's
awful promise, and so she took the tiny baby
away.

The witch called the baby Rapunzel. She
grew into a beautiful girl with long, long hair
as fine as spun gold. When she was sixteen, the
witch took Rapunzel and locked her in a tall

tower so no one would see how beautiful she was. The witch threw away the key to the tower, and so whenever she wanted to visit Rapunzel she would call out, "Rapunzel, Rapunzel, let down your hair," and Rapunzel would throw her golden plait of hair out of the window at the top of the tower so the witch could slowly scramble up.

Now one day it happened that a handsome young prince was riding through the woods. He heard the witch call out to Rapunzel and he watched her climb up the tower. After the witch had gone, the prince came to the bottom of the tower and he called up, "Rapunzel, Rapunzel, let down your hair," and he climbed quickly up the shining golden plait. You can imagine Rapunzel's astonishment when she saw the handsome Prince standing in front of her but she was soon laughing at his stories. When he left, he promised to come again the next day, and he did. And the next, and the next, and soon they had fallen in love with each other.

One day as the witch clambered up, Rapunzel exclaimed, "You are slow! The prince doesn't take nearly as long to climb up the tower," but no sooner were the words out of her mouth than she realized her terrible mistake. The witch seized the long, long golden plait and cut it off. She drove Rapunzel far, far away from the tower, and then sat down to await the prince.

When the witch heard him calling, she
threw the golden plait out of the window.
Imagine the prince's dismay when he sprang
into the room only to discover the horrible
witch instead of his beautiful Rapunzel!
When the witch told him he
would never see his
Rapunzel again, in his

grief he flung himself out of the tower. He fell into some brambles that scratched his eyes so he could no longer see.

And thus he wandered the land, always asking if anyone had seen his Rapunzel. After seven long years, he came to the place where she had hidden herself away. As he stumbled down the road, Rapunzel recognized him, and with a great cry of joy she ran up to him and took him gently by the hand to her little cottage in the woods. As she washed his face, two of her tears fell on the prince's eyes and his sight came back. And so they went back to his palace and lived happily ever after. The witch, you will be pleased to hear, had not been able to get down from the tower, so she did NOT live happily ever after!

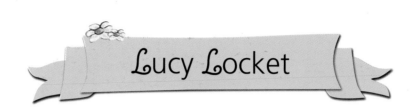

Lucy Locket

Lucy Locket lost her pocket,

Kitty Fisher found it;

There was not a penny in it,

But a ribbon round it.

Peter, Peter

Peter, Peter, pumpkin-eater,

Had a wife and couldn't keep her;

He put her in a pumpkin shell,

And there he kept her very well.

Little Boy Blue

Little Boy Blue,
Come blow your horn,
The sheep's in the meadow,
The cow's in the corn.

But where is the boy

Who looks after the sheep?

He's under a haystack,

Fast asleep.

"Will you wake him?"

"No, not I,

For if I do,

He's sure to cry."

Jack be Nimble

Jack be nimble,

Jack be quick,

Jack jump over the candlestick.

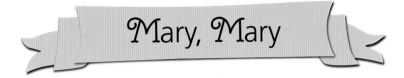

Mary, Mary

Mary, Mary, quite contrary,

How does your garden grow?

With silver bells and cockle shells,

And pretty maids all in a row.

Monday's Child

Monday's child is fair of face,

Tuesday's child is full of grace,

Wednesday's child is full of woe,

Thursday's child has far to go,

Friday's child is loving and giving,

Saturday's child works hard for a living,

And the child that is born on the Sabbath day

Is bonny and blithe, and good and gay.

Peter Piper

Peter Piper picked a peck of pickled pepper;

A peck of pickled pepper Peter Piper picked.

If Peter Piper picked a peck of pickled pepper,

Where's the peck of pickled pepper

Peter Piper picked?

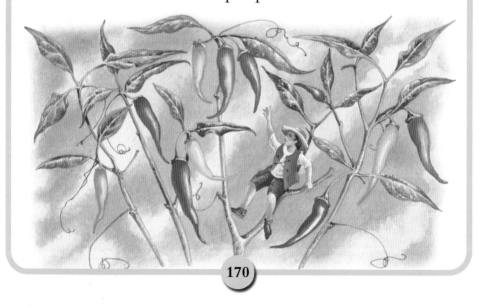

Tom, Tom the Piper's Son

Tom, Tom the piper's son,

Stole a pig and away he run,

The pig was eat,

And Tom was beat,

And Tom went howling

down the street.

Polly, put the Kettle on

Polly, put the kettle on,

Polly, put the kettle on,

Polly, put the kettle on,

And let's have tea.

Sukey, take it off again,

Sukey, take it off again,

Sukey, take it off again,

They've all gone away.

Cinderella

A retelling from the original tale by Charles Perrault

Once upon a time, when there were still fairy godmothers, there was a girl called Cinderella. She lived with her father and his new wife, and her two new step-sisters. The step-mother did not like Cinderella very much, mostly because she was so much nicer than her own two daughters. Cinderella was also much prettier. Oh, but the step-sisters were ugly!

Cinderella had to do all the work in the house as the ugly sisters were also very lazy. They spent all the father's money on new clothes and endless pairs of shoes, and then went off to parties leaving poor Cinderella with piles of stockings to mend.

One day a very grand invitation arrived. The prince was looking for a wife, and had decided to give a ball in three days time for all the young ladies in the land.
The ugly sisters could talk about nothing else. They bought lots of new dresses and many pairs of matching shoes, and then spent every hour trying them all on. They made

Cinderella curl their hair and iron their ribbons and powder their noses. Cinderella was so exhausted running around after them that she had no time to look into her own wardrobe to choose what she should wear.

In a waft of perfume, the ugly sisters swept out of the door into the carriage without as much as a thank you to Cinderella. She closed the door sadly, and went to sit by the fire in the kitchen.

"I wish I could have gone to the ball, too," she sighed.

There was a sudden swirl of stars, and there in front of Cinderella stood an old lady with a twinkle in her eye, and a wand in her hand.

"You shall go to the ball, my dear Cinderella. I am your fairy godmother," she said, smiling. "Now, we must be quick, there is much to do! Please bring me a large pumpkin from the vegetable patch. Oh, and six mice from the barn, and you will find four lizards by the water butt."

Cinderella did as she was bid. With a wave of the wand, the pumpkin was turned into a glittering golden coach and the mice into six pure white horses. The lizards became elegant footmen, dressed in green velvet.

"Now you, my dear," said the fairy godmother, turning to Cinderella. A wave of the wand, and Cinderella's old apron disappeared

and there she stood in a white dress, glittering with golden stars. Her hair was piled on top of her head and it too was sprinkled with stars. On her feet were tiny glass slippers with diamonds in the heels.

"Enjoy yourself, my dear," said the fairy godmother, "but you must leave before midnight for then my magic ends and you will be back in your old apron with some mice and lizards at your feet!"

When Cinderella arrived at the ball everyone turned to look at this unknown beauty who had arrived so unexpectedly. The prince hurried over to ask her to dance and then would not dance with anyone else all evening. The ugly sisters were beside themselves with rage, which of course made them look even uglier.

Cinderella was enjoying herself so much that she forgot the fairy godmother's warning,

so she had a terrible fright when the clock began to strike midnight. She turned from the prince with a cry and ran down the stairs of the palace into her carriage, and disappeared as suddenly as she had arrived. One of the tiny glass slippers with diamonds sparkling in the heels had slipped from her foot as she ran. The prince picked it up and turning to the crowded ballroom declared, "I shall marry the girl whose foot fits this slipper!"

Cinderella, meanwhile, had just managed to reach her garden gate when all her finery disappeared, and by the time the ugly sisters arrived home, both in a towering rage, she was sitting quietly by the fire.

The next morning, the prince went from house to house looking for the mystery girl whose foot would fit the glass slipper. But no one had feet that small. He reached Cinderella's house where first one ugly sister and then the next tried to squash her big feet into the slipper.

"Please let me try," said a quiet voice from the corner, and Cinderella stepped forward. The sisters just laughed in scorn but they soon stopped when they saw that the tiny slipper fitted Cinderella perfectly. There was a sudden swirl of stars, and there in front of Cinderella stood her fairy godmother with a twinkle in her

eye, and a wand in her hand. In an instant, Cinderella was clothed in a gorgeous dress of cornflower blue silk decorated with pearls. On her feet she wore white boots with blue tassels.

The prince whisked Cinderella off to the palace to meet the king and queen, and the wedding took place the very next day. Cinderella forgave the ugly sisters, she was that sort of girl. But the prince insisted the sisters spent one day a week working in the palace kitchens just to remind them how horrid they had been to Cinderella.

What are Little Boys made of?

What are little boys made of?

What are little boys made of?

Frogs and snails and puppy-dogs' tails,

That's what little boys are made of.

What are little girls made of?

What are little girls made of?

Sugar and spice and all things nice,

That's what little girls are made of.

Little Jack Horner

Little Jack Horner

Sat in the corner,

Eating a Christmas pie;

He put in a thumb,

And pulled out a plum,

And said, "What a good boy am I."

Jumping Joan

Here I am,

Little Jumping Joan;

When nobody's with me

I'm all alone.

The Hobby-horse

I had a little hobby-horse,
And it was dapple grey;
Its head was made of pea-straw,
Its tail was made of hay.

I sold it to an old woman
For a copper groat;
And I'll not sing my song again
Without another coat.

Blue Ribbons

Oh, dear, what can the matter be?

Oh, dear, what can the matter be?

Oh, dear, what can the matter be?

Johnny's so long at the fair.

He promised he'd buy me

a bunch of blue ribbons,

He promised he'd buy me

a bunch of blue ribbons,

He promised he'd buy me

a bunch of blue ribbons,

To tie up my bonny

brown hair.

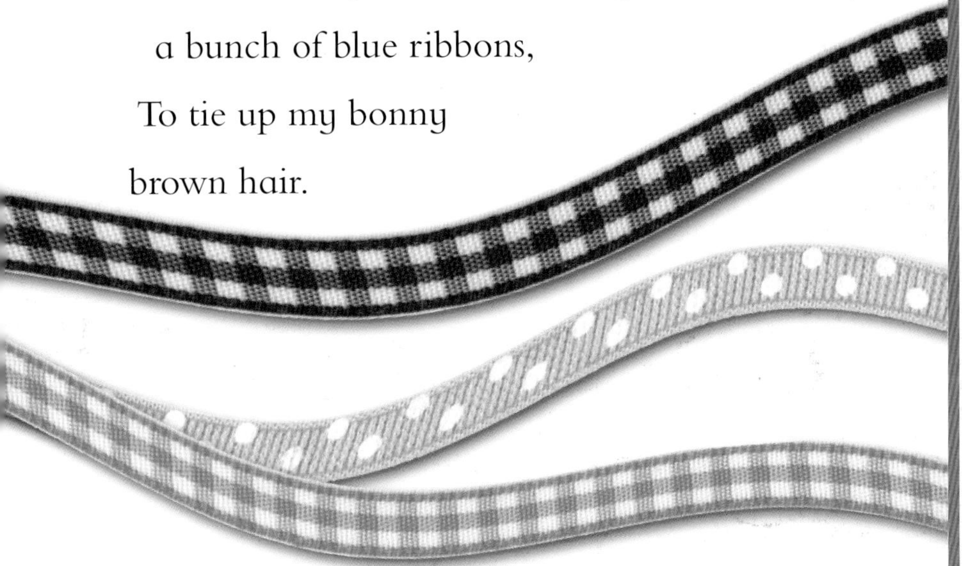

Little Miss Muffet

Little Miss Muffet
Sat on a tuffet,
Eating her curds and whey;

There came a big spider,

Who sat down beside her,

And frightened Miss Muffet away.

Little Girl, Little Girl

Little girl, little girl,
Where have you been?
Gathering roses to give
To the queen.

Little girl, little girl,
What gave she you?
She gave me a
Diamond as big
As my shoe.

Diddle, Diddle, Dumpling

Diddle, diddle, dumpling,

My son John,

Went to bed with his

trousers on;

One shoe off,

and one shoe on,

Diddle, diddle,

Dumpling, my son John.

Little Tommy Tucker

Little Tommy Tucker,

Sings for his supper.

What shall we give him?

White bread and butter.

How shall he cut it

Without a knife?

How will he be married

Without a wife?

Snow White and Rose Red

A retelling from the original story by the Brothers Grimm

Once upon a time there was a widow who had two daughters, Snow White and Rose Red. Snow White was quiet and gentle, Rose Red was wild as the hills, but they loved each other, and their mother, so the little house in the woods was a happy one.

One winter evening as they all sat round the fire there was a knock at the door. Rose Red opened it and gave a scream. There stood a great big brown bear! But in a deep rumbly voice the bear said, "Please do not be afraid. All I ask is that you let me sleep by your fire tonight. It is so cold outside."

"Of course you may shelter with us," said the
mother. And she called the girls to set the soup
on the stove and to put another log on the fire.

"Would you brush the snow from my fur,
please?" asked the bear. Rose Red fetched the
big broom and carefully brushed the bear's great
shaggy coat. Snow White gave him a great bowl
of hot soup and the bear gulped it down in one.
Then he stretched out in front of the fire and
was soon fast asleep.

In the morning, Snow White let him out of the cottage and he padded off into the forest through the deep snow. But in the evening, he returned and once again Snow White and Rose Red and their mother looked after him. After that the bear came every night all through the winter, and they grew very fond of him. But when spring came, the bear told them he would not be returning any more.

"I have to guard my treasure. Once the snows have melted all kinds of wicked people try to steal it," he said and giving them all a hug he set off through the forest. Just as he passed through the garden gate, his fur caught on a nail. For a fleeting moment Snow White thought she saw a glint of gold, but the bear hurried off and was soon out of sight.

A few days later, Rose Red and Snow White were out gathering berries to make jam when

they came alongside a fallen tree. Then they saw
a very cross dwarf, tugging at his beard which
was trapped by the great tree trunk.

"Well, don't stand there like a pair of silly geese! Come and help me!" he shrieked.

Well, no matter how hard they tugged, Rose Red and Snow White were not strong enough to lift the tree, so Rose Red took her scissors out and snipped off the end of the dwarf's beard. He was absolutely furious, and snatched up a big bag of gold from the tree roots and disappeared without a word of thanks.

Some days later the girls' mother said she really fancied a piece of fish for supper, so they went down to the river to see what they could catch. But instead of a fish, there on the bank they found the cross dwarf again. This time his beard was caught up in his fishing line.

"Don't just stand there gawping," he yelled, "help me get free!"

Snow White tried to untangle it but it was impossible, so she too snipped a piece off his beard. He was quite white with rage, but just grasped a casket of jewels that lay at the water's edge and turned away without a word of thanks.

It was the Spring Fair a few days later. The girls decided to go and buy some new ribbons for their hats, and their mother wanted needles for her embroidery, so they set off early in the morning. They had not gone far when they heard a terrible shrieking and crying. They ran towards the sound, and there once more was the cross dwarf, this time struggling in the huge talons of an eagle. They tugged and tugged and the eagle had to let go.

"You have torn my coat," muttered the ungrateful dwarf and picked up a basket of pearls and hobbled off as fast as possible. The girls just laughed and continued on their way to the fair.

They had a wonderful time, and it was quite

late when they walked slowly home. The sun
was just sinking behind a big rock when,
to their astonishment, they came
across the dwarf again. There,
spread out on the ground in

front of him, was a great
pile of gold, precious
jewels and pearls.

Suddenly the dwarf saw
Snow White and Rose Red.
"Go away! Go away! You
horrid girls are always in my
way," he shouted. But just then there
was a huge growl and the great brown bear
stood by their side. With one huge paw he
swiped the dwarf up, up into the sky and no one
ever saw where he fell to earth again. The bear
turned towards Snow White and Rose Red and
as they looked, his great shaggy coat fell away.
There stood a handsome young man, dressed in
a golden suit of the richest velvet.

"Do not be afraid, Snow White and Rose
Red," he said smiling. "Now you can see who I
really am. That wicked dwarf put a spell on me

so he could steal all my treasure, but you have broken the spell by your kindness."

They all went home, laden with the treasure. They talked long into the night, and it was all still true the next morning! Snow White married the handsome young man who, by great good fortune, had a younger brother who married Rose Red, so they all lived happily ever after.

So if you ever find a dwarf with half his beard missing, I would be very careful if I were you.

One, Two, Three, Four, Five

As I was going to St. Ives

As I was going to St. Ives,

I met a man with seven wives.

Each wife had seven sacks,

Each sack had seven cats,

Each cat had seven kits;

Kits, cats, sacks and wives,

How many were going to St. Ives?

Goldilocks and the Three Bears

A retelling from the original tale by Andrew Lang

Once upon a time there was a little girl called Goldilocks who lived in the middle of a great forest with her mother and her father. Now ever since she was tiny, her mother had told her she must never, ever wander off into the forest for it was full of wild creatures, especially bears. But as Goldilocks grew older she longed to explore the forest.

One washday, when her mother was busy in
the kitchen, hidden in clouds of steam,
Goldilocks sneaked off down the path that led
deep into the forest. At first she was happy,
looking at the wild flowers and listening to the
birds singing, but it did not take long for her to
become hopelessly lost.

She wandered for hours and hours and, as it grew darker, she became frightened. She started to cry, but then she saw a light shining through the trees. She rushed forward, sure she had found her way home, only to realize that it was not her own cottage that she was looking at. Even so, she opened the door and looked inside.

On a scrubbed wooden table there were three bowls of steaming hot porridge – a big one, a middle-sized one and a little one. Goldilocks was so tired that she quite forgot all her manners and just sat down at the table. The big bowl was too tall for her to reach. The middle-sized bowl was too hot. But the little one was just right, so she ate all the porridge up.

By the warm fire there were three chairs – a big one, a middle-sized one and a little one. Goldilocks couldn't climb up into the big one. The middle-sized one was too hard. The little was just the right size, but as soon as she sat down, it broke into pieces. Goldilocks scrambled to her feet and then noticed there were steps going upstairs, where she found three beds –

a big one, a middle-sized one and a little one.
The big bed was too hard. The middle-sized one
was too soft. But the little one was just right and
she was soon fast asleep.

The cottage belonged
to three bears, and it was
not long before they
came home. They knew
at once that someone had
been inside.

Father Bear growled, "Who has been eating
my porridge?"

Mother Bear grumbled, "Who has been eating my porridge?"

And Baby Bear gasped, "Who has been eating my porridge, AND has eaten it all up?"

The bears looked round the room. They looked at the chairs by the warm fire.

Father Bear growled, "Who has been sitting in my chair?"

Mother Bear grumbled, "Who has been sitting in my chair?"

And Baby Bear gasped, "Who has been sitting in my chair, AND has broken it to bits?"

The bears went upstairs to look at their beds.

Father Bear growled, "Who has been sleeping in my bed?"

Mother Bear grumbled, "Who has been sleeping in my bed?"

And Baby Bear gasped, "Who has been sleeping in my bed, AND is still there?"

Suddenly Goldilocks woke up. All she could see was three very cross-looking bears. She jumped off the bed, ran down the stairs, and out of the door. She ran and ran and ran, and by good fortune found herself outside her own cottage. Her mother and father scolded her, but then gave her lots of hugs and kisses, and a big bowl of soup. Goldilocks had certainly learnt her lesson, and she never ever wandered off again.

I Saw Three Ships

I saw three ships come sailing by,

Come sailing by, come sailing by,

I saw three ships come sailing by,

On New Year's Day in the morning.

And what do you think was in them then,

Was in them then, was in them then?

And what do you think was in them then,

On New Year's Day in the morning?

Three pretty girls were in them then,

Were in them then, were in them then,

Three pretty girls were in them then,

On New Year's Day in the morning.

Three Blind Mice

Three blind mice, three blind mice,

See how they run! See how they run!

They all ran after the farmer's wife,

Who cut off their tails with a carving knife,

Did you ever see such a thing in your life,

As three blind mice?

Three Men in a Tub

Rub-a-dub-dub,

Three men in a tub;

And who do you think they be?

The butcher, the baker,

The candlestick-maker;

They all jumped out of a rotten potato,

'Twas enough to make a man stare.

I Love Sixpence

I love sixpence, pretty little sixpence,
I love sixpence better than my life;
I spent a penny of it, I spent another,
And I took fourpence home to my wife.

Oh my little fourpence, pretty little fourpence,
I love fourpence better than my life;
I spent a penny of it, I spent another,
And I took twopence home to my wife.

Oh my little twopence, pretty little twopence,
I love twopence better than my life;
I spent a penny of it, I spent another,
And I took nothing home to my wife.

Two Cats of Kilkenny

There once were two cats of Kilkenny,

Each thought there was one cat too many,

So they fought and they fit,

And they scratched and they bit,

Till, excepting their nails

And the tips of their tails,

Instead of two cats, there weren't any.

Six Little Mice

Six little mice sat down to spin;

Pussy passed by and she peeped in.

"What are you doing, my little men?"

"Weaving coats for gentlemen."

"Shall I come in and cut off your threads?"

"No, no, Mistress Pussy, you'd bite off our heads."

"Oh, no, I'll not, I'll help you to spin."

"That may be so, but you don't come in."

Rumpelstiltskin

A retelling from the original tale by the Brothers Grimm

Once upon a time there was a miller. He was a foolish man who was always boasting. Then he went too far.

The king was riding past the mill with his huntsmen one day. The miller's daughter was sitting in the doorway, spinning. The king noticed that she was a pretty girl so he began talking to her. Her father came bustling up and began to tell the king what a splendid daughter she was.

"Why, your Majesty, she can even spin straw into gold!" boasted the ridiculous miller.

Needless to say, the poor girl could do nothing of the sort but the king thought this was

an excellent way to refill the palace treasure
house which was rather empty, so he took her
back to the palace. He put her in a room with a
great pile of straw and told her he wanted to see
it all spun into gold the next morning, or else it
would be the worse for her.

As soon as the door was locked she began to cry. The task was impossible. Then she heard a thin little voice.

"Do stop crying! You will make the straw all wet, and then we will have no chance of turning it into gold!"

There in front of her stood a strange little man. He had a tiny round body with long

skinny legs and huge feet. His
clothes looked as if they
had seen better days, and
on his head he wore a tall
battered-looking hat.

"If you give me your
necklace, I will do what
the king has asked of
you," he snapped.

The miller's
daughter unclasped her
necklace and handed it to the little man. He hid
it deep in one of his pockets, and sat down
by the spinning wheel.

The spinning wheel turned in a blur. The pile
of straw grew smaller, and the mound of shining
gold grew higher. As the first light of day shone
in through the window it was all done.

The strange little man disappeared as suddenly as he had appeared. The king was delighted with the great pile of gold, and asked the miller's daughter to marry him. She was too shy to reply so the king just took her silence as her agreement and married her anyway that afternoon.

For a while all was well. But then the treasure house grew empty again so once more the poor girl, now the queen, was locked in a room with a pile of straw and a spinning wheel.

As the queen wept, once more the strange little man appeared. The queen asked him to help her again, and offered him all the rich jewels she was wearing. But the strange little man was not interested in jewels this time.

"You must promise to give me your first born child," he whispered.

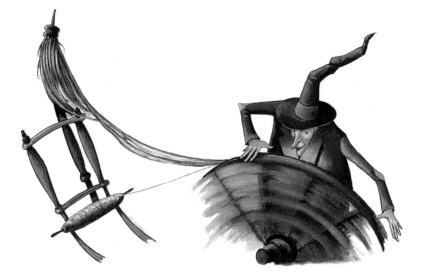

The queen was desperate. But she promised
and the little man sat down at the spinning
wheel. A great pile of gold appeared by the side
of the spinning wheel, and by dawn the straw
had all gone. The king was delighted and for a
while all was well. Then the queen gave birth to
a beautiful baby, and she remembered with
dread her promise to the strange little man.

Seven days after the baby was born, he appeared by the side of the cradle. The queen wept.

"There you go again," said the little man crossly, "always crying!"

"I will do anything but let you have my baby," cried the queen.

"Very well then, anything to make you stop crying," said the little man, who by now was dripping wet from all the queen's tears. "If you can guess my name in three days, I will let you keep your baby," he said and disappeared as suddenly as he had appeared.

The next morning the little man appeared by the side of the cradle. The queen had sent messengers out far and wide to see if anyone knew the strange little man's name.

"Is it Lacelegs?" she asked.

"No!"

"Is it Wimbleshanks?"

"No!"

"Is it Bandyknees?"

"No!"

And the little man disappeared as suddenly as he had appeared. The queen sent out even more messengers to the lands far beyond the borders of the kingdom. The second morning the strange little man appeared by the side of the cradle.

"Is it Bluenose?" the queen asked.

"No!"

"Is it Longtooth?"

"No!"

"Is it Skinnyribs?"

"No!" and the little man disappeared with a nasty laugh.

The queen waited up all night as her messengers came in one by one, and just as she was giving up all hope of saving her precious baby, in came the very last one. He was utterly exhausted but he brought the queen the best of news. In a deep, deep, dark forest he had found a strange little man dancing round a fire, singing this song.

"Today I brew, today I bake,

Tomorrow I will the baby take.

The queen will lose the game,

Rumpelstiltskin is my name!"

When the strange little man appeared again by the cradle, the queen pretended she still did not know his name.

"Is it Gingerteeth?" she asked.

"No!" said the little man, and he picked the baby up.

"Is is Silverhair?" asked the queen.

"No!" said the little man, and he started to walk towards the door, with a wicked smile.

"Is it Rumpelstiltskin?" asked the queen, and she ran up to the strange little man.

"Some witch told you that!" shrieked the little man, and he stamped his foot so hard that he fell through the floor and was never seen again. The queen told the king the whole story and he was so pleased his baby and his queen were safe that he forgot to be cross with the miller who had told such a terrible fib in the first place!

Bonfire Night

Remember remember the fifth of November

Gunpowder, treason and plot.

I see no reason why gunpowder, treason

Should ever be forgot...

Five Little Pussy Cats

Five little pussy cats playing near the door;

One ran and hid inside

And then there were four.

Four little pussy cats underneath a tree;

One heard a dog bark

And then there were three.

Three little pussy cats thinking what to do;

One saw a little bird

And then there were two.

Two little pussy cats sitting in the sun;

One ran to catch his tail

And then there was one.

One little pussy cat looking for some fun;

He saw a butterfly and then there was none.

One, Two, Buckle my Shoe

One, two, buckle my shoe,

Three, four, knock at the door,

Five, six, pick up sticks,

Seven, eight, lay them straight,

Nine, ten, a big fat hen,

Eleven, twelve, dig and delve,

Thirteen, fourteen, maids a-courting,

Fifteen, sixteen, maids in the kitchen,

Seventeen, eighteen, maids

in waiting,

Nineteen, twenty,

my plate's empty.

The Twelve Months

Snowy, Flowy, Blowy,

Showery, Flowery, Bowery,

Hoppy, Croppy, Droppy,

Breezy, Sneezy, Freezy.

George Ellis
1753–1815, b. England

Three Little Kittens

Three little kittens, they lost their mittens,

And they began to cry,

"Oh, mother dear, we sadly fear

That we have lost our mittens."

"What! Lost your mittens, you naughty kittens!

Then you shall have no pie.

Mee-ow, mee-ow, mee-ow.

No, you shall have no pie."

The three little kittens, they found their mittens,

And they began to cry,

"Oh, mother dear, see here, see here,

For we have found our mittens."

"What! Found your mittens, you silly kittens!

Then you shall have some pie."

"Purr-r, purr-r, purr-r,

Oh, let us have some pie."

The Three Billy Goats Gruff

A folk tale from Europe

In a mountain valley beside a rushing river, there lived three billy goats. One was very small, one was middle-sized and one was huge, and they were called the Three Billy Goats Gruff. Every day they would eat the lush green grass by the river, and they were very content.

One day, however, the Three Billy Goats Gruff decided they would like to cross the river and see if the grass was any greener on the other side. The grass was actually no greener, nor was it any tastier, but they all felt they would like a change. First they had to find a way to cross the rushing river. They trotted a good way upstream before they found a little wooden bridge. After a supper of lush green grass, they decided to wait until next morning before crossing the wooden bridge, so they settled down for the night.

Now, what the Three Billy Goats Gruff did not know was that under the little wooden bridge there lived a very mean and grumpy troll. He could smell the Three Billy Goats Gruff,

and he thought they smelled good to eat. So the next morning when the Three Billy Goats Gruff had eaten a breakfast of lush green grass, the troll was hiding under the little wooden bridge, waiting for his chance to have breakfast too.

"That little wooden bridge does not look too strong," said the very small Billy Goat Gruff. "I will go across first to see if it is safe," and he trotted across the little wooden bridge. But when he was only halfway across, the mean and grumpy troll leapt out of his hiding place.

"Who is that trit-trotting across my bridge?"

he roared. "I am going to eat you up!"

But the very small Billy Goat Gruff wasn't ready to be eaten up just yet, so he bravely said to the mean and grumpy troll, "You don't want to eat a skinny, bony thing like me. Just wait till my brother comes across, he is much bigger," and with a skip and a hop, the very small Billy Goat Gruff ran across the bridge to the lush green grass on the other side.

The middle-sized Billy Goat Gruff started to cross the little wooden bridge, but when he was only halfway across, the mean and grumpy troll roared at him.

"Who is that trit-trotting across my bridge?" he roared. "I am going to eat you up!"

But the middle-sized Billy Goat Gruff wasn't ready to be eaten up just yet either, so he bravely said to the mean and grumpy troll, "You don't want to eat a skinny, bony thing like me. Wait till my brother comes across, he is even bigger," and with a skip and a hop, the middle-sized Billy Goat Gruff ran across the bridge to the lush green grass on the other side.

Now, the huge Billy Goat Gruff had been watching all the time. He smiled to himself and stepped onto the little wooden bridge. By this time the troll was very hungry , and he was even meaner and grumpier when he was hungry. He didn't bother to hide, but stood in the middle of the bridge looking at the huge

Billy Goat Gruff who came trotting up to him.

"Who is that trit-trotting across my bridge?" he roared. "I am going to eat you up!"

"Oh no, you won't!" said the huge Billy Goat Gruff, and he lowered his head and with his huge horns he biffed the mean and grumpy troll into the rushing river. The water carried him far away down the river, and he was never seen again. The Three Billy Goats Gruff lived happily for many more years eating the lush green grass, and they were able to cross the river whenever they wanted!

One, Two, Three, Four, Five

One, two, three, four, five,

Once I caught a fish alive.

Six, seven, eight, nine, ten,

Then I let it go again.

Why did you let it go?

Because it bit my finger so.

Which finger did it bite?

This little finger on the right.

The Twelve Dancing Princesses

A retelling from the original story by the Brothers Grimm

The king was very puzzled. He had twelve daughters, each one as beautiful as the moon and the stars, and he loved them above all the riches in his kingdom. But every morning the

princesses would appear yawning and bleary-eyed, and with their shoes worn quite through. Every evening the king would kiss them good night and lock the door behind him. So how did they get out? And where did they go?
The princesses certainly were not letting on.

Buying new shoes every day was costing him a fortune so the king determined to solve the mystery. The court messenger was sent to all four

265

corners of the kingdom to issue the king's proclamation that he would give the hand of one of his daughters in marriage to any man who could discover the secret. But should he fail after three nights he would be banished forever.

Needless to say there were plenty of young men willing to risk banishment to win such a prize. But they soon found the princesses were too clever by half. Before they retired for the night, the princesses sang and played their musical instruments and fed them sweetmeats and rich honeyed mead. Before they realized it morning had come and there were the sleepy princesses and twelve pairs of worn-out shoes.

The king was beside himself. Only the court shoemaker went about with a smile on his face.

Now into the kingdom at this time there wandered a penniless soldier. He read the proclamation and had just decided to try his

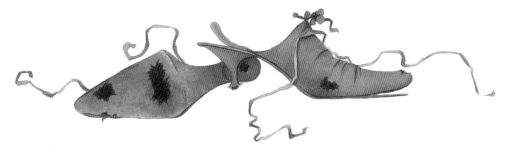

luck when an old woman came slowly down the
dusty road. The young man offered her some of
his bread and cheese, and as they sat peaceably
together the old woman asked where he was
bound. When he had explained she said, "Well, I
may be able to help you. You must not drink the
mead those cunning princesses offer you, for it is
drugged. Pretend to be asleep, and you shall see
what you shall see. This may help you," and the
old woman handed him a silver cloak.
"Whenever you wear this you will be invisible.
Use it well!" and the old woman disappeared.

"Well, perhaps I will succeed now I have magic on my side," murmured the young man as he set off for the palace. By now the king was tearing his hair out. The court shoemaker had taken on extra cobblers to help keep up with the demand for new shoes every day. The princesses were falling asleep into their bowls of porridge at breakfast every morning.

The young man bowed deeply to the king and smiled at all the princesses. He ate a hearty supper but when the eldest princess gave him a goblet of mead he only pretended to drink it. Then he yawned loudly and let his head droop as if he had fallen asleep.

The butler and the first footman dumped the young man onto the bed placed across the door of the princesses' bedchamber. He cautiously opened one eye and gazed around the room. The princesses were putting on gorgeous velvet and brocade dresses and rings and necklaces. They giggled and whispered as they brushed their hair, powdered their faces and then pulled on the brand new jewelled slippers that the shoemaker had only delivered a few hours

earlier. The eldest princess clapped her hands three times. A trap door opened up in the floor and they all swiftly descended down a steeply curving staircase. Just as soon as the last princess had disappeared the young man flung the magic cloak round his shoulders and rushed after them.

He found himself in a wondrous garden where the trees were covered in rich jewels, sparkling in candlelight. Musicians played whirling tunes and he saw all the princesses dancing with the most handsome princes. The young man was spellbound, but he managed to keep his wits about him. He reached up and broke off a branch from one of the jewelled trees and hid it under his cloak. Then he ran back and lay down on his bed as though he had never stirred. So it happened on the second and the third nights.

It was with a weary voice that the king asked the young man at breakfast on the fourth day if he had found out where the princesses went at night. The king sat up very quickly when the young man told his tale and produced the branches from the trees. The king was delighted and the young man chose the youngest sister for his bride. And they all lived happily ever after. Except, of course, the court shoemaker, who always made the young man's shoes just a little too tight so they pinched.

The Elves and the Shoemaker

A retelling from the original story by the Brothers Grimm

There was a time when everyone believed in elves. The shoemaker and his wife in this story certainly did!

The shoemaker worked hard from morn to night. The shoes he made were of the finest leather, but business was slow. One night he found he only had enough leather left for one more pair of shoes. With a heavy heart, he cut the leather carefully and left the pieces ready on his work bench to sew the next morning. He blew out the candle, and crossed the yard from his little shop into the house.

"Wife, I do not know what we shall do. I have just cut out the very last piece of leather in the shop," he said sadly.

"Don't be too gloomy, husband," said his wife with a tired smile. "Perhaps you will be able to sell this last pair of shoes for a fine price."

The next day the shoemaker was up early as usual. When he pulled back the shutters in the shop, you can imagine his surprise when he saw not pieces of leather ready to sew on the bench, but a fine pair of ladies' shoes with delicate pointed toes. The stitching was so fine you would think it had been done by mice. He put the shoes in the window of the shop, and before long a rich merchant came in and bought the shoes for his new wife, paying the poor shoemaker double the usual price. The shoemaker was delighted at this turn in his fortunes, and bought enough leather to make two new pairs of shoes. Once again, he cut the leather, and left the pieces on his work bench to sew the next day.

The next day the shoemaker was up even earlier than usual. His wife came with him as he went into the shop, and pulled back the shutters.

"Oh husband," she gasped, for there on the bench stood two pairs of the finest shoes she had ever seen. There was a green pair with red heels, and a pair so shiny and black the shoemaker could see his face in them. He put the shoes in the window, and very quickly in came a poet who bought the green pair with red heels, and not far behind him there was a parson who bought the shiny black pair. And both paid him a great deal of money for the splendid shoes with stitching so fine you would think it had been done by mice.

This continued for many days. The shoemaker would buy new leather and leave the pieces cut ready on his bench at night, and when he came

back in the morning there would be the most
exquisite shoes. The shoemaker's reputation
spread, and his shop was soon full of customers.
Before long the shoemaker and his wife were no
longer poor, but they still lived simply as they
had little wish for the luxuries of life.

One day, the wife said, "Husband, I think we
must see who it is who has given us this great
good fortune so we may thank them."

The shoemaker agreed, so that night after
laying out the cut leather pieces, he and his wife
hid behind the door of the shop. As the town hall

clock struck midnight, they heard a scampering
of tiny feet and little voices, laughing. Two elves
slid out from behind the skirting board and
climbed onto the bench where they were soon
hard at work, stitching away with tiny stitches
that were so fine they might have been done by
mice. The elves sang as they stitched, but oh!
They looked poor. Their trousers were ragged,
their shirts were threadbare and their feet looked
frozen as they had neither socks nor shoes.

Soon the leather was gone, and on the bench
stood more shoes. The elves slipped away.

The next day, the shoemaker took some
green-and-yellow leather
and made two
little pairs

of boots, yellow with green heels. The wife took some cloth and made two little pairs of red trousers and two green jackets with silver buttons. She knitted two little pairs of socks. That night, they laid out the clothes and boots, and hid behind the shop door.

As the town hall clock struck midnight, the two elves slid out from behind the skirting board and climbed onto the bench. When they saw the gifts, they clapped their hands in delight, flung off their old rags and tried on their new clothes and the boots. They looked splendid. Then they slipped behind the skirting board, and the shoemaker and his wife never saw them again.

But once a year when the shoemaker opened the shop in the morning, on his bench he would find a pair of shoes with stitching so fine you would think it had been done by mice.

Favourite Folk

The Muffin Man

O do you know the muffin man,

The muffin man, the muffin man,

O do you know the muffin man,

Who lives in Drury Lane?

O yes, I know the muffin man,

The muffin man, the muffin man,

O yes, I know the muffin man,

Who lives in Drury Lane.

The Gingerbread Man

An English folk tale

One fine sunny day, an old woman was making some ginger biscuits. She had a little dough left over and so she made a gingerbread man. She gave him raisins for eyes and cherries for buttons, and put a smile on his face with a piece of orange peel. Then she popped him in the oven. But as she lifted the tray out of the oven when the biscuits were cooked, the gingerbread man hopped off the tray and ran straight out of the door! The old woman ran after him, and her husband ran after her, but they couldn't catch the gingerbread man. He called out, "Run, run, as fast as you can! You can't catch me, I'm the gingerbread man!"

The old dog in his kennel ran after the old man and the old woman, but he couldn't catch the gingerbread man. The ginger cat, who had been asleep in the sun, ran after the dog, but she

couldn't catch the gingerbread man. He called out, "Run, run, as fast as you can! You can't catch me, I'm the gingerbread man!"

The brown cow in the meadow lumbered after the cat, but she couldn't catch the gingerbread man. The black horse in the stable galloped after the cow but he couldn't catch the gingerbread man. He called out, "Run, run, as fast as you can! You can't catch me, I'm the gingerbread man!"

The fat pink pig in the sty trotted after the horse, but she couldn't catch the gingerbread man. The rooster flapped and squawked after the pig but he couldn't catch the gingerbread man. He called out, "Run, run, as fast as you can! You can't catch me, I'm the gingerbread man!"

He ran and ran, and the old woman and the

old man, the dog and the cat, the cow and the horse, the pig and the rooster all ran after him. He kept running until he came to the river. For the first time since he had hopped out of the oven, the gingerbread man had to stop running.

"Help, help! How can I cross the river?" he cried.

A sly fox suddenly appeared by his side.

"I could carry you across the river," said the sly fox.

The gingerbread man jumped onto the fox's back, and the fox slid

into the water.

"My feet are getting wet," complained the gingerbread man.

"Well, jump onto my head," smiled the fox, showing a lot of very sharp teeth. And he kept on swimming.

"My feet are still getting wet," complained the gingerbread man again after a while.

"Well, jump onto my nose," smiled the fox, showing even more very sharp teeth.

The gingerbread man jumped onto the fox's nose, and SNAP! the fox gobbled him all up. When the fox climbed out of the river on the other side, all that was left of the naughty gingerbread boy was a few crumbs. So the old woman and the old man, the dog and the cat, the cow and the horse, the pig and the rooster all went home and shared the ginger biscuits. They were delicious.

Mix a Pancake

Mix a pancake,

Stir a pancake,

Pop it in the pan;

Fry the pancake,

Toss the pancake –

Catch it if you can.

Christina Rossetti
1830–94, b. England

There was a Crooked Man

There was a crooked man,

and he went a crooked mile,

He found a crooked sixpence

against a crooked stile,

He bought a crooked cat,

which caught a crooked mouse,

And they all lived together

in a little crooked house.

Old Mother Hubbard

Old Mother Hubbard

Went to the cupboard

To get her poor dog a bone;

But when she came there

The cupboard was bare,

And so the poor dog had none.

The Queen of Hearts

The Queen of Hearts, she made some tarts,

All on a summer's day;

The Knave of Hearts, he stole the tarts,

And took them clean away.

The King of Hearts called for the tarts,

And beat the Knave full sore;

The Knave of Hearts brought back the tarts,

And vowed he'd steal no more.

The Frog Prince

A retelling from the original story by the Brothers Grimm

Once upon a time, there lived a very spoilt princess who never seemed content. The more she had, the more she wanted. And she just would not do as she was told.

One day she took her golden ball out into the woods, although she had been told by her chief nanny that she must embroider some new handkerchiefs. She threw the golden ball high up into the sky once, twice, but the third time it slipped from her hands and, with a great splash, it fell down, down into a deep well. The princess stamped her foot and yelled, but this did not help. So she kicked the side of the well, and was just getting ready for another big yell, when a very large frog plopped out of the well.

"Ugh!" said the princess. "A horrible slimy frog," but the frog didn't move. Instead, it said, "What are you making such a fuss about?"

A talking frog! For a moment the princess was speechless, but then she looked down her nose and said, "If you must know, my golden ball has fallen down this well, and I want it back."

With a sudden leap, the frog disappeared down the well. In the wink of an eye, it was back with the golden ball.

The princess went to snatch it up, but the frog put a wet foot rather firmly on it and said,

"Hasn't anyone taught you any manners? 'Please' and 'thank you' would not go amiss, and anyway I have a special request to make."

The princess looked at the frog in utter astonishment. No one ever dared talk to her like that, and certainly not a frog. She glared at the frog and said crossly, "May I have my ball back, please, and what is your special request?"

The frog did not move its foot, but bent closer to the princess.

"I want to come and live with you in the palace and eat off your plate and sleep on your pillow, please."

The princess looked horrified, but she was sure a promise to a frog wouldn't count so she said, "Of course you can," and grabbed her ball from frog and ran back to the palace very quickly.

That night at supper the royal family heard a strange voice calling,

"Princess, where are you?" and in hopped the frog.

The queen fainted. The king frowned.

"Do you know this frog, princess?" he asked.

"Oh bother!" said the princess again, but she had to tell her father what had happened. When he heard the story, he insisted the princess keep her promise.

The frog ate very little, the princess even less. And when it was time to go to bed, the king just

looked very sternly at the princess who was trying to sneak off on her own. She bent down and picked the frog up by one leg, and when she reached her great four-poster bed, she plonked the frog down in the farthest corner. She did not sleep a wink all night.

The next evening, the frog was back. Supper was a quiet affair. The queen stayed in her room,

the king read the newspaper, and the princess tried not to look at the frog. Bedtime came, and once again the frog and the princess slept at opposite ends of the bed.

The third evening, the princess was terribly hungry so she just pretended the frog was not there and ate everything that was placed in front of her. When it came to bedtime, she was so exhausted that she fell in a deep sleep as soon as her head touched the pillow.

The next morning when she woke up, she felt much better for her good sleep until she remembered the frog. But it was nowhere to be seen. At the foot of the bed, however, there stood a handsome young man in a green velvet suit.

"Hello, princess. Do you know that you snore?" he said.

The princess's mouth fell open ready to yell, but the handsome young man said, "I don't suppose you recognize me, thank goodness, but I was the frog who rescued your golden ball. I was bewitched by a fairy who said I was rude and spoilt," and here the young man looked sideways

at the princess whose mouth was still hanging open, "And the spell could only be broken by someone equally rude and spoilt having to be nice to me."

The princess closed her mouth. The king was most impressed with the young man's good manners, and the queen liked the look of his fine green velvet suit. Everyone liked the fact that the princess had become a very much nicer person. Before long it seemed sensible for the princess and the handsome young man to get married. They had lots of children who were not at all spoilt and everyone lived happily ever after. The golden ball and the green velvet suit were put away in a very dark cupboard.

Old King Cole

Old King Cole was a merry old soul,

And a merry old soul was he;

He called for his pipe, and he called for his bowl,

And he called for his fiddlers three.

Every fiddler, he had a fine fiddle,

And a very fine fiddle had he;

Oh, there's none so rare as can compare

With King Cole and his fiddlers three.

Bobby Shaftoe

Bobby Shaftoe's gone to sea,

Silver buckles on his knee;

He'll come back and marry me,

Bonny Bobby Shaftoe!

Bobby Shaftoe's young and fair,

Combing down his yellow hair;

He's my love for evermore,

Bonny Bobby Shaftoe!

The Old Woman who Lived in a Shoe

There was an old woman

who lived in a shoe,

She had so many children

she didn't know what to do.

She gave them some broth
without any bread;
She whipped them all
soundly and put
them to bed.

Thumbelina

Retold from the original tale by Hans Christian Andersen

Once upon a time there was a woman who wanted more than anything in the world to have a child – but she didn't know where to get one. She went to see a witch about it and the witch gave her a special seed. The woman planted the seed in a flowerpot and it grew . . . and grew . . . and grew . . . into a bud that looked very much like the bud of a tulip. "What a beautiful flower!" the woman murmured one day, and she leant over and kissed the closed petals. POP! the bud exploded into an open flower, and there sitting in the middle of it was a tiny little girl, no bigger than the woman's thumb. The woman was overjoyed with her beautiful daughter and named her Thumbelina. The woman thought that her tiny daughter was utterly delightful and looked after her tenderly. But one night, a big, fat toad came hopping through a broken pane of glass in the woman's window. Hmmm, thought the toad, as her bulging eyes caught sight of Thumbelina sleeping in half a walnut shell. She would make a perfect wife for my son. The toad picked up the dreaming little girl, bed and all, and hopped away to the marshy river where she lived. The toad swam out

to where the water ran fast and deep and placed
Thumbelina in her walnut shell on a broad, flat
lily pad. Now you can't run away, the toad
thought, and she swam off to break the good
news to her son . . .

When Thumbelina woke up and saw that she
was not only lost, but trapped too, she began to
cry bitterly. The fish wiggled up to see what was
causing all the tiny splashes
and ripples, and they
took pity on the
sad, tiny girl.
Quickly and
silently, they
nibbled through the
lily pad's green stem
and Thumbelina went floating
down the river.

Soon, she was far out of the toads' reach . . .

and still the lily pad raft floated on. Thumbelina sailed past towns and was swept out into the countryside. Thumbelina liked it among the fields. It was sunny and peaceful, and a pretty white butterfly fluttered down to keep her company. Suddenly a large flying beetle dive-bombed the lily pad and wrapped his legs around Thumbelina's tiny waist. In a flash, Thumbelina found herself sitting on a twig with the beetle high up in a tree, watching her lilypad drift away without her.

Hundreds of the beetle's curious friends came crawling out of the bark to peer at what he had brought home. "Urgh! Look, it's only got two legs," the beetle children squealed.

"Where are its feelers?" some of the lady beetles murmured.

"Hasn't it got a slim bottom?" other lady beetles gasped in horror, admiring their own round shiny ones.

"It is ugly," the male beetles had to admit. "Let's get rid of it." And they flew down from the tree with Thumbelina and sat her on a daisy.

Poor Thumbelina felt very like crying. But just then she noticed a little hole in the earth below her that looked very like it was a type of doorway. She jumped down from the daisy and peered into the gloom. "Hello!" she cried. "Is anyone at home?"

After a few seconds, out popped a fieldmouse's head. She looked Thumbelina up and down, and tutted loudly. "Dear, dear!" the fieldmouse scolded. "You look exhausted and hungry. If you're as lost as you look, you're very welcome to stay here with me – in return for keeping my rooms nice and clean and tidy."

So all winter Thumbelina lived with the fieldmouse. Every day, she washed and swept

and scoured and polished, and the fieldmouse
was very kind to her. Although, truth to tell,
Thumbelina found life rather boring. The
fieldmouse wasn't at all skilled at making
entertaining conversation and neither was her
regular visitor, Mr Mole. He came once every
week in his fine black velvet overcoat, but he
didn't like to talk. He just enjoyed sitting and
peering at Thumbelina through his little, short-
sighted eyes, and listening to her sing.

The fieldmouse was
delighted that her
friend so liked
Thumbelina. "I think
he's falling in love
with you," she
whispered to
Thumbelina
excitedly.

The fieldmouse was even more sure that she was right when Mr Mole invited them both to visit him in his splendid underground mansion.

"I have dug a tunnel from your house to mine," Mr Mole informed them, "so you may come and see me in comfort. Only please close your eyes when you are halfway down the passage, for I am afraid that a dead swallow is lying there."

Thumbelina wasn't at all revolted when she came across the dead bird on her first trip to Mr Mole's house. Instead, she felt pity for the poor thing, lying all stiff and still on the cold earth. While the fieldmouse ran on eagerly ahead, Thumbelina bent down and stroked the bird's feathers. "Goodbye, sweet swallow," she murmured, and she laid her head on the bird's soft breast. DUP! DUP! DUP! Thumbelina heard the swallow's heart beating – only very faintly, but Thumbelina knew that the bird was still just alive!

From then on, Thumbelina found as many excuses as possible to creep away from the fieldmouse and into the tunnel to care for the swallow. Over the weeks that followed, she placed leaves under the bird's head and plaited a coverlet of hay to keep it warm. She dripped drops of water into its weak throat and fed it tiny morsels of food – and gradually the swallow began to recover. By the time the weather had begun to grow warmer, the swallow was well enough to stand and hop about. On the first day of spring, the swallow was totally better – and extremely grateful for all Thumbelina's kindness.

"One day, I will repay you," he twittered as he hopped up the passageway and soared off into the blue sky.

It was then that the fieldmouse announced to

Thumbelina that she had arranged for her to be married to Mr Mole. "He is very wealthy and will take good care of you," the fieldmouse beamed.

But Thumbelina was horrified. "I cannot live my life underground!" she cried, and ran sobbing out into the fields. She held her hands up to the sunshine and looked all around at the flowers, and she felt as if her heart would break.

Just then, Thumbelina heard a familiar twittering above her head. She looked up and saw her friend the swallow swooping down towards her. "Come away with me," cried the swallow, "I know a place where you will be happy. I have seen it on my travels." Joyfully, Thumbelina jumped onto his soft, feathery back.

The swallow flew off with Thumbelina over villages and roads, lakes and forests, snow-capped mountains, to a land where the weather

was always sunny, where the breeze was always
warm, and where in every flower there lived a
tiny person just like Thumbelina. Thumbelina
was very happy in her new home. She even
married a handsome prince who lived in a
rosebud and who was extremely glad that she
had never become Mrs Mole!

Best of all, the swallow came to visit every
year in September, and stayed with Thumbelina
and her prince each winter long.

Humpty Dumpty

Humpty Dumpty sat on a wall,

Humpty Dumpty had a great fall;

All the king's horses and all the king's men

Couldn't put Humpty together again.

It's Raining

It's raining, it's pouring,

The old man is snoring,

He went to bed and

bumped his head,

And couldn't get up in

the morning.

Rain

The rain is falling all around,

It falls on field and tree,

It rains on the umbrellas here,

And on the ships at sea.

Robert Louis Stevenson
1850–94, b. Scotland

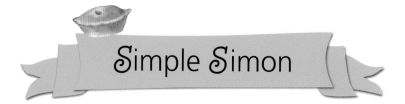

Simple Simon

Simple Simon met a pieman,

Going to the fair;

Says Simple Simon to the pieman,

"Let me taste your ware."

Says the pieman to Simple Simon,

"Show me first your penny."

Says Simple Simon to the pieman,

"Indeed I have not any."

There was an Old Woman

There was an old woman tossed up in a basket,

Seventeen times as high as the moon;

And where she was going

I couldn't but ask it,

For in her hand she

carried a broom.

"Old woman, old woman, old woman," said I,

"O whither, O whither, O whither so high?"

"To sweep the cobwebs off the sky!

And I'll be with you by and by."

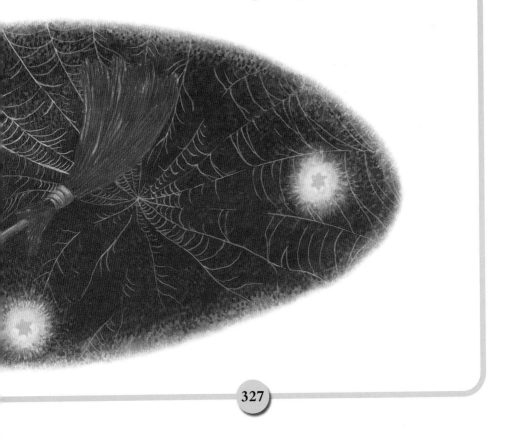

Curly Locks

Curly Locks, Curly Locks,

Wilt thou be mine?

Thou shalt not wash dishes,

Nor yet feed the swine;

But sit on a cushion,
And sew a fine seam,
And feed upon
   strawberries,
Sugar and cream.

Doctor Foster

Doctor Foster went to Gloucester

In a shower of rain;

He stepped in a puddle,

Right up to his middle,

And never went there again.

Yankee Doodle

Yankee Doodle came to town,

Riding on a pony;

He stuck a feather in his cap

And called it macaroni.

Yankee doodle, doodle do,

Yankee doodle dandy,

All the lasses are so smart,

And sweet as sugar candy.

Little Polly Flinders

Little Polly Flinders
Sat among the cinders,
Warming her pretty little toes.

Her mother came and caught her,
And whipped her
little daughter
For spoiling her
nice new clothes.

Duke of York

Oh, the grand old
Duke of York,
He had ten thousand men;
He marched them up to the
top of the hill,
And he marched
them down again.

And when they were up they were up,

And when they were down they were down.

And when they were only half-way up,

They were neither up nor down.

The Emperor's New Clothes

Retold from the original tale by Hans Christian Andersen

There was once an emperor who loved new clothes above everything else. Designers, tailors, clothmakers, dyers, and specialists in all sorts of needlework travelled to his city from all over the world. Anyone who could suggest flashy, fancy new outfits for the emperor was always very welcome at the palace.

One day, it was the turn of two weavers to be quickly ushered into the emperor's dressing room. The emperor, his butler and all his Officers of the Royal Wardrobe, gasped with amazement as they listened to them describe their work.

"We have created a special fabric that is so light and airy the wearer cannot feel it," the first weaver announced.

"Our samples are top secret, which is why we have not been able to bring any to show you," the second weaver explained.

"However we can assure you that not only are our designs and patterns exquisitely beautiful," said the first weaver, "but the fabric has the unique advantage that it is completely invisible to anyone not worthy of his job –"

"– or who is just plain stupid!" laughed the second weaver, and the emperor and all his courtiers gasped and chuckled along.

"We would be honoured if you would like to order the very first suit made out of this extraordinary fabric, your imperial majesty," said the first weaver, bowing low.

The emperor clapped his hands with delight.

"I'd like to place an order right away!" he commanded, and he gave the two weavers a large sum of money so that they could buy the rare, expensive materials they needed and begin their work without delay.

The weavers set up their looms in the palace studio and got going right away. News of the strange cloth spread round the city like wildfire and soon everyone was talking about it. But the weavers worked behind closed doors and no one got even a glimpse of what they were doing. Still, day and night everyone heard the looms clicking and the shuttles flying, and work on the magical cloth seemed to be progressing well.

As the days went on, the emperor began to
feel rather uneasy about seeing the cloth for the
first time. Imagine if I can't see the fabric myself!
he thought to himself. How dreadfully
embarrassing that would be! The worried
emperor decided to send his trusted old butler to
see how the weavers were getting on. He was
sure that his butler was both fit for his job and
very wise, and would be sure to see the
wonderful material.

The weavers bowed low and ushered the
butler into the studio. But the butler couldn't see

anything at all. Heavens above! the butler thought to himself. Those looms look totally bare to me! I must either be a very bad butler, or else I'm an idiot. No one must ever find out . . . So he praised the material that he could not see, told the king that the weavers' work was indeed magnificent, and everyone in the city heard that the cloth was truly unbelievable!

Soon afterwards, the weavers sent word to the emperor that they needed more money to buy essential items for the work. The emperor had been so delighted with the butler's report that he sent them twice as much money as before. The emperor was more excited than ever. "I'm going to have the most amazing suit of clothes in the world!" he giggled to himself ten times a day.

Eventually, just as the impatient emperor thought he was going to explode with waiting, the weavers announced their work was finished.

They went to the dressing room to present the material to the emperor amid fanfares of trumpets. "Is the cloth not beautiful beyond all imagining?" the weavers sighed.

The emperor smiled a wide smile, trying to hide his horror. All that the weavers appeared to be holding up before him was thin air. The emperor's worst fear had come true – to him the cloth was invisible! I cannot be thought to be a fool or not worthy to be ruler, the despairing emperor thought. So he beamed and leant forwards and inspected the air. "Wonderful! Splendid! Magnificent!" he cried, and his butler and all the Officers of the Royal Wardrobe nodded and cried out compliments. None of them could see anything either, but they weren't about to risk losing their jobs by admitting it.

So the weavers got out their tape measures and their scissors and they set about cutting the thin air (or so it seemed) into a pattern. All night long they sewed with needles that appeared to have no thread, and in the morning they announced that the emperor's new clothes were ready. "If your majesty would care to disrobe, we will dress you in the amazing garments."

The emperor swallowed hard and took off all his clothes. The weavers helped him on with the underpants and trousers and shirt and jacket that he couldn't see. "Aren't they lighter than cobwebs?" they sighed. The emperor spluttered his agreement. He couldn't feel that he had any clothes on at all.

The emperor stood back and looked at himself in the mirror. According to what he saw, he didn't have a stitch on! But he turned this way and that, pretending to admire himself. And the butler and all the Officers of the Royal Wardrobe cried out, "How wonderfully the new clothes fit you, sire!" and "We have never seen the like of the amazing colours!" and "The design is a work of genius!" – even though it looked to them as if the emperor was as naked as the day he was born.

Everyone else can see my new suit except me, the emperor thought to himself glumly. And he walked out of the palace to parade before the people in his marvellous new clothes.

The streets were lined with hundreds of people

who ooohed! and aaaahed! over the emperor's invisible new clothes – for none of them wanted to admit that they couldn't see them.

Suddenly, a little boy's shrill voice rose over the applause of the crowd. "But the emperor has nothing on!" the child shouted. "Nothing on at all!" Suddenly there was a stunned silence and

the little boy found that hundreds of pairs of eyes were staring at him. Then someone sniggered ... someone else tried to stifle a giggle ... another person guffawed and snorted ... and the whole crowd burst out into uncontrollable peals of laughter.

The emperor's face turned as red as a ripe tomato. "I am indeed a fool!" he murmured. "I have been swindled by two tricksters!" He ran back to the palace as fast as his short, naked legs could carry him – but the clever (and now very rich) weavers were long gone!

The Sorcerer's Apprentice

A German folk tale

The sorcerer lived in a dusty room at the top of a very tall gloomy tower. His table was covered with bottles and jars full of strange-coloured potions, and bubbling mixtures filled the air with horrible smells. The walls of the tower were lined with huge old books. These were the sorcerer's spell books and he would let no one else look inside them.

The sorcerer had a young apprentice called Harry. He was a good but lazy boy who longed only to be able to do magic himself. The sorcerer had promised to teach him all he knew, but only when he thought Harry was ready.

One day the sorcerer had to visit a friend who was a warlock. The sorcerer had never left Harry alone in the tower before and he did not entirely trust him. Looking very fierce, the sorcerer gave Harry his instructions.

"I have a very important spell to conjure up tonight when I return, so I need the cauldron full of water from the well," he said. "When you have filled the cauldron, you can sweep the floor and then you must light the fire."

Harry was not best pleased. It would take many, many trips to the well to fill the cauldron, and he would have all those steps to climb each time. Perhaps the sorcerer could read his mind, for the last thing he said as he climbed out of the window to fly away on his small green dragon was, "Touch nothing!" and off he flew in a cloud of smoke and flame from the dragon.

Harry watched until the sorcerer was safely far out of sight, and then did precisely what he had been told not to do. He took down one of the old dusty spell books. For a while all was quiet in the tower, and then Harry found what he was looking for. It was a spell to make a broomstick obey orders. Harry didn't hesitate. He forgot the sorcerer's instructions, he forgot that magic can be very dangerous. He took the broomstick in one hand and the spell book in the other, and read out the spell in a quavery voice for, truth to tell, he was very nervous. Nothing happened. Harry tried again, and this time his voice was stronger.

The broomstick quivered and then stood up. It grabbed a bucket and jumped off down the stairs. Soon it was back, the bucket brimful of water which it tipped into the cauldron. Harry was delighted and smiled as the broomstick set off down the stairs again. Up and down the broomstick went and soon the cauldron was full.

"Stop, stop!" shouted Harry, but the broomstick just carried on, and on.

Soon the floor was awash and then the bottles and jars were floating around the room. Nothing Harry could say would stop the broomstick, and so in desperation, he grabbed the axe that lay by the fireside and chopped the broomstick into pieces. To his horror, the pieces of wood turned into new broomsticks and set off downstairs to the well, buckets appearing in their hands.

By now the water was nearly up to the ceiling. Wet spell books spun round and round the room, and Harry gave himself up for lost. Suddenly there was a great clatter of wings and a hiss of steam as the green dragon flew into the tower. The sorcerer was back! In a huge voice he commanded the broomsticks to stop. They did. Then he ordered the water back into the well. It all rushed back down the stairs. Then he ordered the dragon to dry everything with its hot breath. Then he turned to look at Harry. And, oh dear! Harry could see that the sorcerer was very, very angry indeed. The sorcerer looked as if he might turn Harry into something terrible, but then he sat down on a soggy cushion with a squelch. "Right, I think it is time I taught you how to do magic PROPERLY!" And he did.

The Lion and the Mouse

A retelling from Aesop's Fables

The lion was very hungry. As he padded through the tall grass, something rustled by his feet. He reached out a great paw, and there was a squeak. He had caught a tiny mouse by the tail.

"Oh please let me go, dear lion," cried the tiny mouse. "I should be no more than a single mouthful for you. And I promise I will be able to help you some day."

The lion roared with laughter. The thought of a tiny mouse being able to help such a huge creature as himself amused him so much that he did let the mouse go.

"He would not have made much of a meal

anyway," smiled the lion.

The mouse scuttled away, calling out to the
lion, "I shall not forget my promise!"

Many days and nights later the lion was
padding through the tall grass again when he
suddenly fell into a deep pit. A net was flung
over him, and he lay there helpless, caught by
some hunters. He twisted and turned but he
could not free himself. The hunters just laughed
at his struggles and went off to fetch a cart to
carry the great lion back to their village.

As he lay there, the lion heard a tiny voice in his ear.

"I promised you I would be able to help you one day."

It was the tiny mouse! And straight away he began to gnaw through the rope that held the lion fast. He gnawed and chewed, and chewed and gnawed, and eventually he chewed and gnawed right through the rope and the lion was free. With a great bound, he leapt out of the pit

and then reached back, very gently, to lift the tiny mouse out too.

"I shall never forget you, mouse. Thank you for remembering your promise and saving me," purred the great lion.

So the tiny mouse was able to help the great lion. One good turn deserves another, you see?

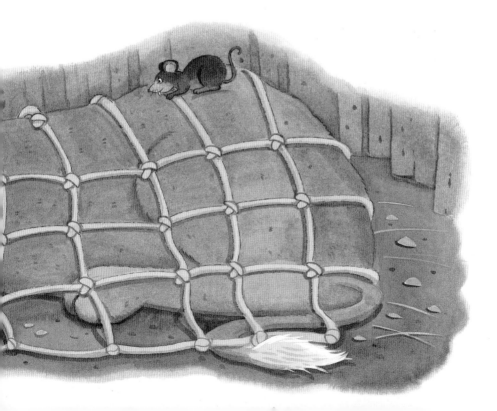

Best-Loved

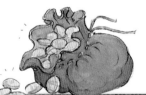

Rain, Rain

Rain, rain, go away,

Come again another day;

Little Tommy wants to play.

Whether the Weather

Whether the weather be fine,

Or whether the weather be not,

Whether the weather be cold,

Or whether the weather be hot,

We'll weather the weather

Whatever the weather,

Whether we like it or not!

Author unknown

As I was Going Out

As I was going out one day
My head fell off and rolled away.
But when I saw that it was gone,
I picked it up and put it on.

And when I got into the street
A fellow cried, "Look at your feet!"
I looked at them and sadly said,
"I've left both asleep in bed!"

Hot-cross Buns

Hot-cross Buns!

Hot-cross Buns!

One a penny, two a penny,

Hot-cross Buns!

Hot-cross Buns!

Hot-cross Buns!

If you have no daughters

Give them to your sons.

I had a Little Nut Tree

I had a little nut tree, nothing would it bear

But a silver nutmeg and a golden pear;

The King of Spain's daughter came to visit me,

And all was because of my little nut tree.

I skipped over water, I danced over sea,

And all the birds in the air couldn't catch me.

The Little Turtle

There was a little turtle,

He lived in a box.

He swam in a puddle,

He climbed on the rocks.

He snapped at a mosquito,

He snapped at a flea.

He snapped at a minnow,

And he snapped at me.

He caught the mosquito,

He caught the flea.

He caught the minnow,

But he didn't catch me.

Vachel Lindsay
1879–1931, b. USA

The Hare and the Tortoise

Retold from the original fable by Aesop

The day that Tortoise challenged Hare to a race, all the animals laughed so hard that their tummies ached. But Tortoise was fed-up with Hare whizzing round him all the time, teasing him about how slow he was. I'll show that Hare, if it's the last thing I do! Tortoise promised himself.

Hare thought that Tortoise's little joke was extremely funny. For that's all Hare thought it was – a joke. Hare never expected that Tortoise would actually go through with his mad idea. So his eyes nearly popped out of his head when he arrived at the starting line to see Tortoise already there, limbering up in a very slow, stiff, creaky sort of way.

"Be careful there, old chap!" Hare worried, as he realized his friend was serious. "You don't want to do yourself an injury."

"Don't worry about me," replied Tortoise. "You should be working out how you're going to beat me. Ha! You won't see me for dust!"

A huge crowd of animals had gathered to watch the race and they all cheered and clapped and jumped up and down at Tortoise's bold remark.

Suddenly, Hare started to feel rather annoyed. "All right then. If that's the way you want it!" he snapped. "I was going to give you a headstart, but obviously you won't be wanting one."

"No need," breezed Tortoise, although his little heart was pumping inside his shell. "First one to the windmill's the winner."

Hare peered into the distance. The windmill was three fields away. He could get there in less than a minute without losing his breath. But surely it would take Tortoise all day to reach it!

"Three! Twit-Two! One!" cried Barn Owl, and Tortoise lifted one leg over the starting line amid thunderous applause.

The stunned Hare watched in amazement as Tortoise began to crawl slowly away. Well, you have to hand it to Tortoise! Hare thought, seeing

the funny side of things again. He's certainly got
a good sense of humour and a lot of guts!

Hare sat down next to the starting line
under a shady tree. It was a beautiful
sunny day and it was very pleasant to
sit there in the dappled light,
watching Tortoise amble
peacefully into the field.
Hare's eyes shut and his head
drooped before he even
realized he was sleepy . . .

Meanwhile, Tortoise
was remembering

what his mum had told him as a child: Slow and steady does it, son. Slow and steady does it. And Tortoise kept on going and didn't give up . . .

Hare didn't wake up until the night air was so cold that it was freezing his whiskers. Where am I? he thought. And then suddenly he remembered the race. Hare leapt to his feet and squinted into the moonlight, but there was no sign of Tortoise. All at once, he heard a faint sound of cheering coming from a long way off, and he saw tiny dark figures jumping up and down around the windmill. "Surely not!" Hare gasped, and shot off over the fields like an arrow. He arrived at the windmill just in time to see all the animals hoisting Tortoise – the champion! – on their shoulders. And of course, after that, Hare never ever teased his friend about being slow again.

Lavender's Blue

Lavender's blue, dilly, dilly,
Lavender's green,
When I am king, dilly, dilly,
You shall be queen.

Who told you so, dilly, dilly,
Who told you so?
'Twas mine own heart, dilly, dilly,
That told me so.

Call up your men, dilly, dilly,
Set them to work,
Some to the plough, dilly, dilly,
Some to the fork.

Some to make hay, dilly, dilly,
Some to reap corn,
Whilst you and I, dilly, dilly
Keep ourselves warm.

Roses are red, dilly, dilly,
Violets are blue;
Because you love me, dilly, dilly,
I will love you.

Sing a Song of Sixpence

Sing a song of sixpence,
A pocket full of rye;
Four-and-twenty blackbirds,
Baked in a pie.

When the pie was opened,
The birds began to sing;
Was not that a dainty dish,
To set before the king?

The king was in his counting-house,

Counting out his money;

The queen was in the parlour,

Eating bread and honey.

The maid was in the garden,

Hanging out the clothes,

When down came a blackbird,

And pecked off her nose.

The North Wind doth Blow

The north wind doth blow,

And we shall have snow,

And what will poor robin do then,

poor thing?

He'll sit in a barn,

And keep himself warm,

And hide his head under his wing,

poor thing.

Who has seen the Wind?

Who has seen the wind?

Neither I nor you:

But when the leaves hang trembling,

The wind is passing through.

Who has seen the wind?

Neither you nor I:

But when the trees bow down their heads,

The wind is passing by.

Christina Rossetti
1830–94, b. England

Christmas is Coming

Christmas is coming,

the geese are getting fat;

Please to put a penny

in the old man's hat;

If you haven't got a penny,

ha'penny will do.

If you haven't got a ha'penny,

God bless you.

If all the Seas were One Sea

If all the seas were one sea,

What a great sea that would be!

If all the trees were one tree,

What a great tree that would be!

If all the axes were one axe,

What a great axe that would be!

And if all the men were one man,

What a great man that would be!

And if the great man took the great axe

And cut down the great tree

And let it fall into the great sea,

What a splish-splash that would be!

The Little Mermaid

Retold from the original tale by Hans Christian Andersen

Far, far out in the ocean, the water is as blue as cornflowers and deeper than the tallest mountain. It is there that the sea-people live, and in the very deepest waters lies the Sea King's palace of coral and mother-of-pearl. The Sea King's beloved wife had died, so his mother, the old queen, took care of his six beautiful mermaid daughters. All day long, the princesses sang and danced, swimming in and out of the pillars and halls of the palace. Sometimes shy, brightly coloured fish swam up to eat out of their hands. And at other times, each would tend the little garden that she cared for in the royal grounds. Each mermaid princess gave her garden its own particular style and design: one was shaped like a whale; another had a rockery of shells; yet another had flowerbeds where the sea-horses came to graze. But the youngest mermaid's garden was shaped like the sun that shone on the world above the sea, and the flowers that grew there blazed red and orange and yellow like the sunlight.

The little mermaid had never been up to the ocean's surface and seen the upper world, for the princesses were only allowed to do so when they reached fifteen years old. But the little mermaid longed for that day to come. She loved to hear the stories her grandmother told of people and

ships and cities
and animals and
meadows and forests
and the like. And
many a night the little
mermaid stood at her
open chamber window,
peering up at the watery
reflections of the moon and the
stars and the dark shapes of ships as
they passed like clouds above her.

When each of her sisters came of age, the little
mermaid begged them eagerly to tell her
everything they had seen. Then at last, she
turned fifteen and it was her turn to see the
upper world for herself.

The little mermaid thought it was more
beautiful than she had ever imagined. Her head
broke through the foam when the sun had just

gone down and the clouds looked as if they were on fire with red and gold. The sound of music and singing was coming from a tall-masted ship bedecked all about with coloured flags and banners. Suddenly rockets zoomed up from it into the sky which exploded into stars that fell glittering all around her – the little mermaid had never seen fireworks before. When she was lifted up on the swell of the sea, she saw onto the ship's magnificent deck and understood the reason for the wonderful celebrations: it was the birthday party of a prince, more handsome than any merman she had ever seen.

As the little mermaid gazed with delight at the prince and his ship, she heard a familiar rumbling stirring deep within the sea. A storm was coming! All at once the sky darkened. Sheets of rain lashed the ship. The waves towered into mountains that hurled the ship upwards and sent it crashing down towards the depths. The little mermaid saw with alarm that the ship wouldn't be able to hold out against the might of the weather and the ocean, and she ducked under the waves as wooden planks and other pieces of the ship came flying out of the darkness at her head. Through the murky waters, the little mermaid was horrified to see human bodies come floating down around her – and among them was her beautiful prince, choking and gasping for air.

The little mermaid shot through the water and clutched him close to her, and began swimming up to the light until his head was above water. The little mermaid hauled the exhausted prince to the shore and let the waves wash him onto the sand, and she stayed in the foam and watched him until the storm

had died away and the morning sunlight came
streaming warmly through the clouds. Then she
saw the green hills for the first time and heard
the peal of bells, and she saw a group of young
girls come skipping out of a white building with
a cross on the top. One of the girls noticed the
prince where he lay. She ran to him and laid his
head in her lap, and slowly the prince opened his
eyes. He looked up at the girl and smiled, and
the little mermaid turned away sadly, for she
knew the prince thought it was that girl who
had rescued him. Down, down, down, the little
mermaid dived into the deeps – and her heart
ached all the way back to her father's palace.

From that moment on, the little mermaid was
thoughtful and sad. She longed to see her
handsome prince again, to tell him that she
loved him and wanted to be with him forever.
She wanted to be human more than anything
else in the whole world. There was only one
thing she could do: make the dangerous journey
to the cold, dark depths of the ocean to see the
Water-Witch.

The Water-Witch's lair
was set about with the
skeletons of
humans she had
drowned and
the remains of
ships she had
wrecked. The
little mermaid
trembled with fear

as she explained why she had come.

"What you long for is extremely difficult to give," the Water-Witch cackled.

"I can make your tail disappear and give you legs so that you can walk about with the humans in the world above. But every step you take will be as painful as if you are treading on knives. And I cannot make your prince fall in love with you. It is up to you, and you alone, to do that. If your prince marries another, the morning afterwards your heart will break and you will turn to foam on the water."

The little mermaid shuddered, but she bade the Water-Witch continue.

"The price for such strong magic is very high," spat the witch. "Once I have given you legs, there is no changing your mind. You will never be able to return to the sea as a mermaid to see your family . . . And there is one more thing. I cannot mix the potion you need unless you give me your voice."

The little mermaid longed so badly for her prince and for a human soul that she whispered, "So be it." The words were the last sounds she ever uttered. For then the Water-Witch took the little mermaid's voice and brewed up an evil-smelling potion for her in exchange.

The little mermaid felt as if her heart would break with grief as she swam back past her father's palace, leaving her sleeping family for the world above. She splashed onto the sand, half-choking through her tears and half-gasping for air, and looked at her beautiful silvery fishtail for the last time. Then the little mermaid raised the witch's brew to her lips and drank deeply. At once pain wracked her body and she fell into a dead faint . . .

The little mermaid awoke to find her

handsome prince standing over her, looking worried. "Are you all right?" he asked, but the little mermaid couldn't reply. Instead, she smiled as she looked down at her body and saw that she had the prettiest pair of legs she could have wished for. Falteringly, she stood up for the very first time. The little mermaid put out her foot – and it was true, each step was like treading on knives. But soon she was dancing and running and skipping along the beach for joy, and the prince was utterly enchanted.

The prince took his new little friend back to the palace and dressed her in fine robes of silk and satin. He didn't seem to mind that she was dumb, and kept her by his side at all times, calling her "my beautiful little foundling".

Yet although the little mermaid was happier than she had ever dreamed was possible, there was a sadness in her eyes and a heaviness in her

heart. Each night, she
would creep out of the
palace and go down to
the seashore.
Sometimes she saw her
sisters way out among
the surf, and they would
sing to her sadly as they
floated on the waves. Once,
she even thought she
glimpsed the golden crowns of her father and
grandmother – but perhaps it was just the
moonlight glinting on the water.

Eventually a day came when the prince led
the little mermaid onto a fine ship just like the
one from which she had rescued him. They
sailed for a night and a day, and all the time the
little mermaid longed to leap into the waves and
dive down to see her family far below. The ship

finally arrived in the harbour of a neighbouring kingdom, and all the people lined the streets to meet them, waving flags and cheering. "See how they welcome me," the prince whispered to the little mermaid. "For today I am going to marry their princess."

The little mermaid felt as if someone had grabbed her heart with icy fingers. Surely it couldn't be true? But when the prince's bride came running down the palace steps to meet him, the little mermaid understood. It was the girl who had found him on the beach; the girl whom the prince thought had saved him from the sea; the girl whom the prince thought was the little mermaid.

That afternoon, the little mermaid stood in church dressed in silk and gold, holding the bride's train. And all the way back to the ship, she cried silent, dry tears.

That night, as the splendid ship floated on the waves, there were flags and fireworks and music and dancing – and the little mermaid felt no more a part of the celebrations than she had when she had watched the prince's birthday party from afar.

The little mermaid stood on the deck all night and listened to the sighing of the sea. She felt the warm night wind on her face and her hair floated in the damp sea mists. When the first rays of the dawn lit up the horizon, the little mermaid prepared herself to dissolve into foam on the waves. But instead, she saw transparent beings of light flying to her through the air. They lifted her up on their wings and soared off into the sky, and the little mermaid found that she was one of them. "We are the daughters of the air," the beautiful beings explained.

"We do not have an immortal soul, but if we perform enough acts of goodness and kindness, we will one day win one for ourselves. And this is your reward for the suffering you have endured."

The little mermaid raised her hands towards the sun and the tears in her eyes were tears of joy. She looked down upon the prince and his bride on their ship. They were searching for her sadly in the water, thinking she had fallen overboard. But the little mermaid didn't stay to watch them for long. She blew them a kiss and flew onwards with the daughters of the air.

Dance to your Daddie

Dance to your daddie,

My bonnie laddie,

Dance to your daddie,

my bonnie lamb;

You shall get a fishie,

On a little dishie,

You shall get a herring when

the boat comes home.

Dance to your daddie,

My bonnie laddie;

Dance to your daddie,

and to your mammie sing;

You shall get a coatie;

And a pair of breekies,

You shall get a coatie when

the boat comes in.

Red Sky at Night

Red sky at night,

Shepherd's delight;

Red sky in the morning,

Shepherd's warning.

O Dear, what can the Matter be?

O dear, what can the matter be?

Dear, dear, what can the matter be?

O dear, what can the matter be?

Johnny's so long at the fair.

He promised to bring me a basket of posies,

A garland of lilies, a garland of roses,

A little straw hat, to set off the ribbons

That tie up my bonny brown hair.

Little Robin Redbreast

Little Robin Redbreast sat upon a tree,

Up went Pussy-cat, down went he,

Down came Pussy-cat, away Robin ran,

Says little Robin Redbreast,

"Catch me if you can!"

Little Robin Redbreast jumped upon a spade,

Pussy-cat jumped after him,

and then he was afraid.

Little Robin chirped and sang,

and what did Pussy say?

Pussy-cat said, "Mew, mew, mew,"

and Robin flew away.

The Owl and the Pussy-cat

The Owl and the Pussy-cat went to sea

In a beautiful pea-green boat,

They took some honey, and plenty of money,

Wrapped up in a five-pound note.

The Owl looked up to the stars above,

And sang to a small guitar,

"O lovely Pussy! O Pussy, my love,

What a beautiful Pussy you are,

you are, you are!

What a beautiful Pussy you are!'

Pussy said to the Owl, "You elegant fowl!

How charmingly sweet you sing!

O let us be married! Too long have we tarried:

But what shall we do for a ring?"

They sailed away, for a year and a day,

To the land where the Bong-tree grows

And there in a wood a Piggy-wig stood

With a ring at the end of his nose,

his nose, his nose,

With a ring at the end of his nose.

"Dear Pig, are you willing to sell for one shilling

Your ring?" Said the Piggy, "I will."

So they took it away, and were

married next day

By the Turkey who lives on the hill.

They dined on mince, and slices of quince,

Which they ate with a runcible spoon;

And hand in hand, on the edge of the sand,

They danced by the light of the moon,

the moon, the moon,

They danced by the light of the moon.

Edward Lear
1812–88, b. England

Pease Pudding

Pease pudding hot,

Pease pudding cold,

Pease pudding in the pot,

Nine days old.

Some like it hot,

Some like it cold,

Some like it in the pot,

Nine days old.

Over the Hills

Tom, he was a piper's son,

He learned to play

when he was young,

And all the tune that

he could play

Was 'over the hills and a

great way off,

The wind shall blow

my top knot off'.

Blow, Wind, Blow

Blow, wind, blow, and go, mill, go,

That the miller may grind his corn;

That the baker may take it,

And into bread make it,

And bring us a loaf in the morn.

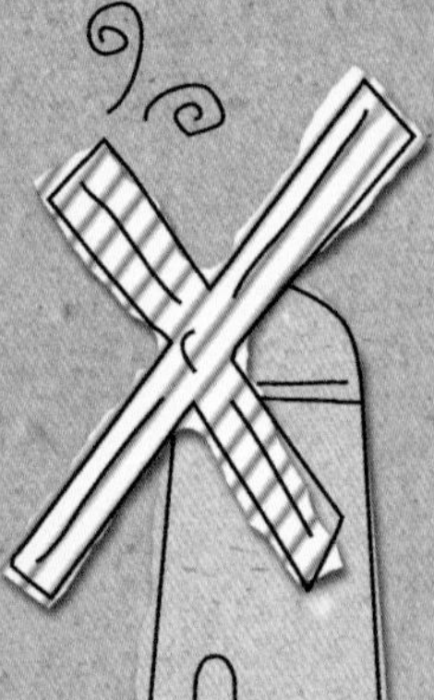

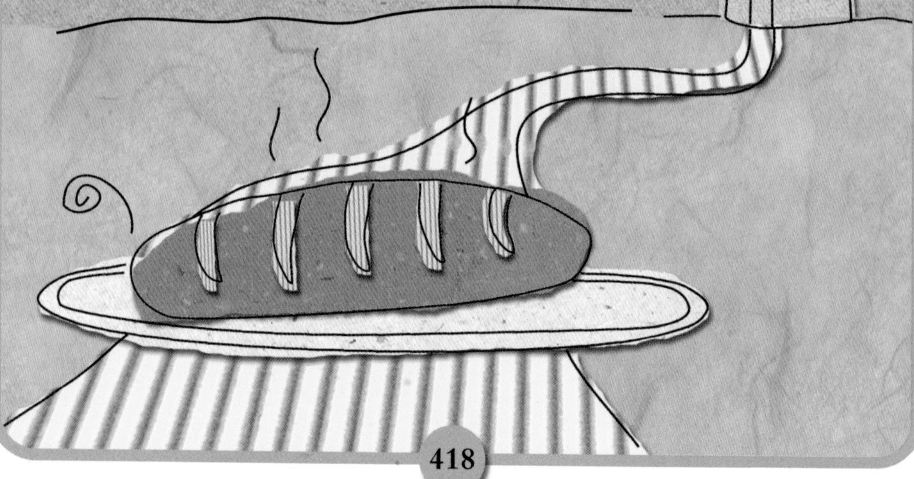

If all the World were Paper

If all the world were paper,

And all the sea were ink,

If all the trees

Were bread and cheese,

What should we have to drink?

London Bridge is Falling Down

London Bridge is falling down,

Falling down, falling down,

London Bridge is falling down,

My fair lady.

Chicken Licken

An English folk tale

One fine day Chicken Licken went for a walk in the woods. Now Chicken Licken was not very bright, and he was also rather inclined to act first and think after. So when an acorn fell on his head, he decided immediately that the sky must be falling in. He set off as fast as he could to tell the king. On the way he met Henny Penny and Cocky Locky.

"I am off to tell the king that the sky is falling in," he clucked importantly.

"We will come too," said Henny Penny and Cocky Locky.

So Chicken Licken, Henny Penny and Cocky Locky set off to find the King. On the way they met Ducky Lucky and Drakey Lakey.

"We are off to tell the king that the sky is falling in," clucked Chicken Licken importantly.

"We will come too," said Ducky Lucky and Drakey Lakey.

So Chicken Licken, Henny Penny, Cocky Locky, Ducky Lucky and Drakey Lakey all set off to find the king. On the way they met Goosey Loosey and Turkey Lurkey.

"We are off to tell the king that the sky is falling in," clucked Chicken Licken importantly.

"We will come too," said Goosey Loosey and Turkey Lurkey.

423

So Chicken Licken, Henny Penny, Cocky Locky, Ducky Lucky, Drakey Lakey, Goosey Loosey and Turkey Lurkey all set off to find the king. On the way they met Foxy Loxy.

"We are off to tell the king that the sky is falling in," clucked Chicken Licken importantly.

"What a good thing I met you all," said Foxy Loxy with a cunning smile. "I know the way, follow me."

So Chicken Licken, Henny Penny, Cocky Locky, Ducky Lucky, Drakey Lakey, Goosey Loosey and Turkey Lurkey all set off behind Foxy Loxy. He led them all straight to his den where he ate every single one of them for his dinner! So the king never heard that the sky was falling in. (It didn't, of course.)

I always Eat my Peas with Honey

I always eat my peas with honey;

I've done it all my life.

They do taste kind of funny

but it keeps them on my knife.

Anonymous

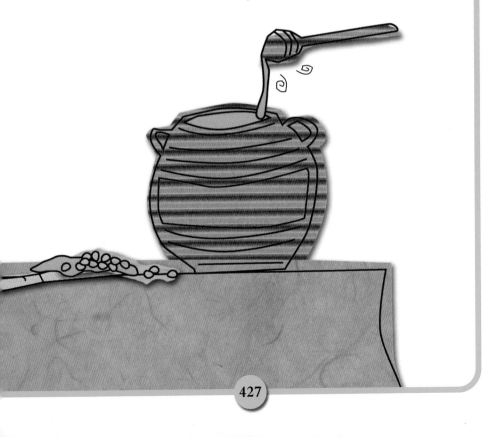

Dick Whittington and his Cat

An English myth

Hundreds of years ago there lived a poor orphan boy called Dick Whittington. His only possession was his cat, but everyone in his village looked after him, so he never wanted for a meal or clothes on his back. In return, he worked hard wherever he was needed. Now Dick's greatest dream was to visit the great city of London where, he had heard, the streets were paved with gold.

One day, a waggoner pulled into the village to give his two great shire horses a drink. Dick offered to rub the horses down, and before long he was telling the waggoner all about his dreams of visiting London town.

"Well, you must be in luck today," smiled the waggoner, "for that is where I am bound. Why don't you come with me and I will drop you off back here again when I return tomorrow?"

This was too good an offer to refuse, so Dick and his cat waved goodbye to the villagers and set off with the waggoner for London. When they arrived, Dick looked round about in astonishment. Never before had he seen such huge buildings, all crowded so closely together. And there were so many people! Dick set off to explore, promising the waggoner he would be back in the evening.

The pavements certainly did not appear to be made of gold. But he kept on thinking he should just try round the next corner, and then the next and, before long, Dick realised that he was hopelessly lost. He stumbled into a

doorway, and worn out with hunger and worry at not keeping his promise to help the waggoner, he fell fast asleep.

Now as luck would have it, Dick had chosen a very good doorway to sleep in. The house belonged to a rich merchant, Mr Fitzwarren, who was kind and willing to help anyone in need. So when he came home later that evening, Mr Fitzwarren took Dick and his cat indoors and told the cook to give him supper. The cook was very grumpy at having to prepare a meal late at night for Dick who, she thought, looked like a ragamuffin.

The next morning, Dick told Mr Fitzwarren the whole story. Smiling, Mr Fitzwarren told Dick that, as he had found, the streets of London were not paved with gold, and indeed life there was hard.

"But you look like a strong boy, would you like to work for me, Dick?" he asked. "You will have a roof over your head and a good dinner every day in return for helping in the kitchen and the stables."

Dick was delighted, and soon settled into the household. He worked hard, and everyone liked him, except the cook. She gave him all the horrible jobs in the kitchen and would let him have a moment's rest. But she didn't dare defy her master so Dick had a good dinner every day.

Whenever one of Mr Fitzwarren's ships went to sea, it was custom for everyone in the household to give something to the ship's cargo for luck. Dick had only his cat. He sadly handed her over.

The ship was at sea for many months before

they came to port in China. The captain and crew went ashore to show the emperor their cargo. The emperor had known the captain for years and they were old friends, so they sat down to a banquet before discussing business. But to the emperor's embarrassment, the meal was ruined by the rats that ran everywhere, even over the plates they were eating off. The emperor explained that they had tried everything but nothing could rid the court of the plague of rats. The captain smiled.

"I think I have the answer," he said and he sent for Dick's cat. Within moments of her arrival, there were piles of dead rats at the emperor's feet. He was so impressed that he gave the captain a ship full of gold just for the cat.

Back in London, Dick's life was a misery. The cook was nastier than ever and he didn't even have his beloved cat for company, so one day he ran away, intending to walk home to his village. But he had not gone far before he heard the church bells ringing, and they seemed to say,

"Turn again Dick Wittington,
Thrice Lord Mayor of London."

Dick didn't know what the bells meant, but he remembered how kind Mr Fitzwarren had been, so he turned round again and went back before the cook had even noticed that he was missing. Of course when the ships came home, Mr Fitzwarren gave Dick his fair share and more. This was the start of Dick's prosperity, and he even married Mr Fitzwarren's daughter, Jane. He did become Lord Mayor of London three times, but he never forgot his early days of poverty and he founded schools and hospitals for the poor. He and Jane had many children, and there were always lots of cats in their great house as well!

Snow White and the Seven Dwarfs

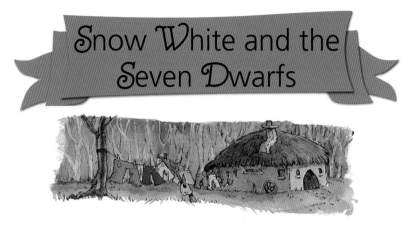

A retelling from the original tale by the Brothers Grimm

The queen was sitting at the window sewing, and thinking about her baby who would be born soon. As she sewed she pricked her finger, and red blood fell on the snow by the ebony window ledge.

"I wish that my daughter be as white as snow, as black as ebony and as red as blood," she said to herself, and so it happened. Her tiny daughter had snow-white skin, lips as red as blood and hair as black as ebony, so she was called Snow

White. But the queen died and the king married again. His new wife was very beautiful but she had a cold heart, and she did not love Snow White.

Every morning the new queen would look into her magic mirror and say,

"Mirror, mirror on the wall

Who is fairest in the land?"

and the mirror would always reply, "Thou, oh queen, Thou art fairest in the land."

So the queen was content. Seven years passed and Snow White grew into a lovely young girl, with her mother's gentle nature.

One morning the queen looked into her mirror as usual, but the mirror's reply filled her with a deep envy.

"Thou, oh queen,
Thou art indeed fair
But Snow White is the fairest in the land."
She ordered her woodsman to kill Snow White. But he could not bear to do such a wicked deed so he hid Snow White deep in the forest. Poor Snow White wandered about until she was utterly weary.

Suddenly, she caught sight of a light through the trees in the distance. It came from a little house with a lantern glowing in one small window. The door swung open at her touch, so she stepped inside. Everything was as neat as a new pin. A scrubbed wooden table was set, with seven plates and seven cups. Seven little chairs were ranged round the fireplace, and along the back wall there were seven little beds, each with a brightly coloured blanket.

There was a basket of logs beside the fireplace, and Snow White soon had a cheerful fire going. She sat in one of the little chairs and before long was fast asleep.

Now the cottage belonged to seven dwarfs and when they came home that evening, they were very worried to discover Snow White fast asleep. They tiptoed round preparing their supper, but as the wonderful smell of stew filled the room, Snow White awoke with a start. She was very surprised to see seven little faces

looking at her, but soon she was telling them
how she came to be in the forest. They were
very angry when they heard about the wicked
queen.

"Might I stay with you?" asked Snow White.
"I could look after you, and have supper ready
for you every night."

The dwarfs were just delighted with this
suggestion, and immediately set about making
Snow White her own chair by the fireside and
her own bed.

Back in the castle, the queen looked into her
mirror in the morning, and asked,

"Mirror, mirror on the wall,

Who is fairest in the land?"

But you can imagine her rage when the
mirror replied,

"Thou, oh queen, Thou art indeed fair,

But Snow White with the seven dwarfs does

dwell and she is fairest in the land."

So the wicked queen disguised herself as an old pedlar, and searched out the dwarfs' cottage. Snow White did not recognize the queen and invited her in.

"Goodness me, you need new laces for your dress," said the old woman, and she pulled the new laces so tightly that Snow White was unable to breathe.

When the dwarfs came home that evening, they were horrified to discover Snow White lying on the floor as if dead. They lifted her up and, of course, saw the laces. They quickly cut the tight cord and the colour came back to Snow White's cheeks.

"Now you know the queen will stop at nothing," they cried. "You must not let anyone indoors again."

The queen looked in her mirror the next morning, and went white with rage when it told her Snow White was still the fairest in the land. She disguised herself as a gypsy, selling wooden pegs and combs. Snow White remembered what the dwarfs had said and would not open the door. But the gypsy passed one of the combs through the window, and the minute it touched her hair, Snow White fell down in a faint for the comb was poisoned.

When the dwarfs came home and found Snow White, they immediately suspected the queen. They found the comb and pulled it  out, and Snow White sat up, quite recovered. They pleaded with her to be more careful the next morning when they set off for work.

So when a farmer's wife appeared at the door trying to sell apples, Snow White would not even open the window.

"Why, anyone would think I was trying to poison you," said the farmer's wife, who was, of course, the wicked queen in disguise.

"I only want to give you some apples. Look how juicy they are!" and she took a big bite out of one.

So Snow White thought it
must be all right and she took
the apple. But the queen had
poisoned it on one side only,

and the minute Snow White took a bite
she fell down dead.

This time when the dwarfs came home, there
was nothing they could do. Snow White was
indeed dead. They could not bear to bury her in
the cold earth so they placed her in a glass
coffin. They wrote her name on the side in silver
and put the coffin in a sheltered part of the
forest, and planted wild flowers all round about.

When the queen looked into her mirror the
next morning, it gave her the answer she
wanted.

"Thou, oh queen,
Thou art fairest in the land."
Years passed. Snow White lay in her coffin,

looking as beautiful as ever. The dwarfs watched over her, and one day they found a young prince kneeling by the side of the glass coffin. He had fallen in love with Snow White the moment he had set eyes on her. When the dwarfs saw how deeply the prince felt about their beloved Snow White, they agreed that he take the glass coffin to his palace where he wished to set it in his rose gardens.

As the prince lifted the glass coffin, the piece of poisoned apple flew from her lips, and Snow White opened her eyes. She saw the prince, she saw her faithful dwarfs and she cried, "Where am I? What has happened?"

There was huge excitement as everyone tried to talk at once.

The prince wasted no time and asked Snow White to marry him. She agreed as long as the dwarfs could come and live at the palace as well, and they all lived happily ever after.

But what of the queen? She looked in her mirror the morning Snow White and the prince were to be married.

"Mirror, mirror on the wall
Who is fairest in the land?"
The mirror replied,
"Snow White, oh queen,
Snow White who marries her prince today,
She is fairest in the land."

The queen was so ugly in her rage that the mirror cracked from side to side. And she was never able to look in a mirror ever again as long as she lived.

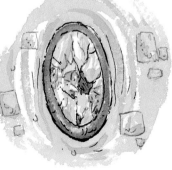

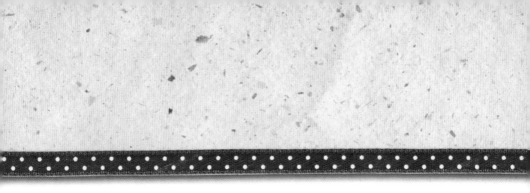

Time for Bed

Rock-a-bye Baby

Rock-a-bye baby,

On the tree top.

When the wind blows

The cradle will rock;

When the bough breaks

The cradle will fall.

Down will come baby,

Cradle and all.

Sleeping Beauty

A retelling from the original tale by Charles Perrault

Long, long ago, when fairies were still able to grant wishes, there lived a king and queen who wanted, more than anything in the whole world, to have a baby daughter. When their wish was finally granted and a beautiful tiny princess lay in her cradle, the king and queen decided to

have a great candlelit party to celebrate. They
invited the twelve most important fairies in the
land and a great many other people besides.

As well as the thousands of glittering candles, there were golden tables piled high with all kinds of delicious food, and the royal orchestra played their most cheerful tunes. The twelve fairies all lined up to present their christening gifts to the tiny princess. Their gifts were those that only a fairy can give: beauty, kindness, grace, honesty and the like. The princess smiled happily in her cradle as one by one the fairies tiptoed up.

The eleventh fairy had just promised the princess a sweet singing voice, when there was a great roll of thunder and all the candles flickered out. There stood quite the most wicked fairy anyone had ever seen. She was dressed all in black, her long straggly hair was black and her eyes, glittering in rage, were as black as the crow's feathers. Her voice was like a saw as she screeched, "How dare you not invite me to the party! I too have a gift for the little princess," and she smiled a not very nice smile. "Because you have forgotten me, my gift is that when the princess is sixteen she shall prick her finger on a spindle and die!" and with a horrid laugh, the wicked fairy disappeared.

As the candles were hastily relit, everyone started talking at once. Then a quiet voice was heard over all hubbub. It was the twelfth fairy.

"I cannot undo this wicked spell," she whispered, "but I can decree that the princess will not die. She will instead fall into a deep sleep for a hundred years," and all the fairies slipped away leaving the court in despair.

The king, of course, immediately ordered that all the spinning wheels in the land were to be burned. After a while, everyone grew less frightened, and as the princess grew up into the most lovely girl, the wicked fairy's prediction slipped from most people's memories.

On her sixteenth birthday the princess went exploring. At the top of a tower she did not remember seeing before, she found an old woman, sitting at a spinning wheel.

It was, of course, the wicked fairy in disguise.
The princess was fascinated and, as she bent
forward to look at the cloth, her hand caught
the sharp spindle and she immediately fell to the
ground as though dead. With a swirl of smoke
and a nasty laugh, the wicked fairy disappeared.

Everyone else in the palace fell asleep at the
same moment. The king fell asleep with his
ministers, the queen and her maids fell asleep in
her dressing room. The cook fell asleep in the
kitchen in the middle of baking a cake, the
groom fell asleep as he fed the horses in the
stables and even the little linnet the princess had
in a golden cage by her bedside fell asleep on its
perch. A great high thorn hedge grew up and
soon the palace was completely hidden. Time
stood still and all was silent.

Many, many years passed. The tale of
the sleeping princess spread far and wide,

and many came to try to find her. But no one could get through the thorn hedge. And so after even more years, people forgot what lay behind the hedge.

Then one day a handsome prince came riding through the woods, and as he reached the thorn hedge, thousands of pink roses burst into bloom. The prince walked forward, and a path appeared leading through the hedge towards the palace. It was a hundred years to the day since the princess had pricked her finger. The prince was astonished by the sight that met his eyes. Everywhere people lay asleep, frozen in the midst of whatever they had been doing when the spell caught them.

The prince climbed the tower, and there he found the princess, looking as lovely as ever. He bent over and kissed her, and immediately the spell was broken. The king and his ministers carried on just where they had left off. The queen chose which dress she wanted to wear and the maids brushed her hair. The cook put her cake in the oven and the groom led the horses out into the courtyard. And even the little linnet in her golden cage sang a joyful song.

As for the princess . . . ! Well, she and the prince had fallen in love with each other on the spot, and were married the very next day. They all lived happily ever after, and the wicked fairy was never ever seen again.

Twinkle, Twinkle, Little Star

Twinkle, twinkle, little star,

How I wonder what you are.

Up above the world so high,

Like a diamond in the sky.

Come, let's to Bed

Come, let's to bed, says Sleepy-head;

Sit up awhile, says Slow;

Bang on the pot, says Greedy-gut,

We'll sup before we go.

To bed, to bed, cried Sleepy-head,

But all the rest said No!

It is morning now,

You must milk the cow,

And tomorrow to bed we go.

Hush, Little Baby

Hush, little baby, don't say a word,
Papa's going to buy you a mocking bird.

If the mocking bird won't sing,
Papa's going to buy you a diamond ring.

If the diamond ring turns to brass,
Papa's going to buy you a looking-glass.

If the looking-glass get broke,
Papa's going to buy you a billy-goat.

If that billy-goat runs away,
Papa's going to buy you another today.

Father's Day

Walk a little slower, Daddy,
Said a little child so small.
I'm following in your footsteps
And I don't want to fall.

Sometimes your steps are very fast,
Sometimes they are hard to see;
So, walk a little slower, Daddy,
For you are leading me.

Someday when I'm all grown up,
You're what I want to be;
Then I will have a little child
Who'll want to follow me.

And I would want to lead just right,

And know that I was true;

So walk a little slower, Daddy,

For I must follow you.

Author unknown

Sleep, Baby, Sleep

Sleep, baby, sleep,
Thy father guards the sheep;
Thy mother shakes the dreamland tree
And from it fall sweet dreams for thee,
Sleep, baby, sleep.

Sleep, baby, sleep,
Our cottage vale is deep;
The little lamb is on the green,
The woolly fleece so soft and clean
Sleep, baby, sleep.

Sleep, baby, sleep,

Down where the woodbines creep;

Be always like the lamb so mild,

A kind and sweet and gentle child,

Sleep, baby, sleep.

The Princess and the Pea

A retelling from the original story by Hans Christian Andersen

The prince was very fed up. Everyone in the court, from his father, the king, down to the smallest page, seemed to think it was time he was married. Now the prince would have been very happy to get married, but he did insist that his bride be a princess, a real true and proper princess. He had travelled the land and met

plenty of nice girls who said they were
princesses, but none, it seemed to him, were
really true and proper princesses. Either their
manners were not quite exquisite enough,
or their feet were much too big. So he
sat in the palace, reading dusty
old history books and getting
very glum.

One night, there was the most terrible storm. Rain was lashing down, and thunder and lightning rolled and flashed round the palace. The wind kept blowing out the candles, and everyone huddled closer to the fire. Suddenly there was a great peal from the huge front door bell.

And there, absolutely dripping wet, stood a princess. Well, she said she was a princess, but never did anyone look less like a princess. Her hair was plastered to her head, her dress was wringing wet and her silk shoes were covered in mud. She was quite alone, without even the smallest maid, and just where had she come from? But she kept insisting she was a princess.

We will see about that, thought the queen. While the dripping girl sat sipping a mug of warm milk and honey, the queen went to supervise the making of the bed in the second-best spare bedroom. She didn't think it necessary to put their late night visitor in the best spare bedroom, after all she might only be a common-or-garden duchess. The queen told the maids to take all the bedclothes and the mattress off the bed. Then she placed one single pea right on the middle of the bedstead. Next the maids piled twenty mattresses on top of the pea, and then twenty feather quilts on top of the mattresses. And so the girl was left for the night.

In the morning, the queen swept into the bedroom in her dressing gown and asked the girl how she had slept.

"I didn't sleep a wink all night." said the girl. "There was a great, hard lump in the middle of the bed. It was quite dreadful. I am sure I am black and blue all over!"

Now everyone knew she really must be a princess, for only a real princess could be as soft-skinned as that. The prince was delighted, and insisted they got married at once, and they lived very happily ever after. They always slept in very soft beds, and the pea was placed in the museum, where it probably still is today.

Bye Baby Bunting

Bye baby bunting,

Father's gone a hunting,

To get a little rabbit-skin,

To wrap his little baby in.

How many Miles to Babylon?

How many Miles
to Babylon?
Three score and ten.
Can I get there
by candlelight?
Aye, and back again.
If your feet are
nimble and light,
You'll get there
by candlelight.

Ladybird, Ladybird

Ladybird, ladybird,
fly away home,
Your house is on fire and
your children are gone,

All except one and that's
little Ann, for she crept
under the frying pan.

Wee Willie Winkie

Wee Willie Winkie
runs through the town,
Upstairs and downstairs
in his nightgown,
Rapping at the window,
crying through the lock,
"Are the children in their beds,
for it's now eight o'clock?"

Star Light, Star Bright

Star light, star bright,

First star I see tonight,

I wish I may, I wish I might,

Have the wish I wish tonight.

Aladdin and the Lamp

A tale from The Arabian Nights

Aladdin's father had died years ago, abandoning Aladdin with no education, no job and no money. And so Aladdin lived life as a street urchin until there was a knock at his mother's door one evening and in strode a tall, turbaned man with a flowing cloak and the longest moustache Aladdin had ever seen.

"May Allah be praised! At last I have found

you both!" the man cried, smiling broadly at Aladdin's mother. "I am Aladdin's long-lost uncle, a wealthy merchant, and I offer my nephew Aladdin the chance to come and work for me and make his fortune."

At this, Aladdin's mother's eyes opened wide and round. "I'm sure your father never mentioned a brother," she hissed under her breath to her son. "But don't be so foolish as to point it out!" And she set about making the merchant truly welcome.

Next morning, Aladdin was horrified to find that he was woken up at sunrise, forced to wash and tidy his hair, and pushed out of doors to begin his new career. Still half-asleep, he ran to keep up with his so-called uncle as he strode at a cracking pace through the bazaar, past the harbour, and right into the burning hot desert. "Find some wood and build a fire," his uncle

ordered,
and from
the tone of his voice,
Aladdin thought it was best not to
argue. His uncle scattered some
strange-smelling powders into the
flames and chanted words in a
weird language. There was
a blaze of green fire and
the ground trembled.
When the smoke cleared, a
trapdoor had appeared in the earth.

Aladdin's uncle heaved it open and
bellowed at Aladdin, "Go down and
find me lamp!"

Aladdin was frozen with fear. His
teeth chattered and his knees knocked
with terror at all that had happened.

"You useless boy!"

Aladdin's uncle roared, sounding highly like Aladdin's mother. He took a ring from his hand and shoved it roughly onto Aladdin's finger.

"This magic ring will keep you safe. Now go!" And he pushed Aladdin through the trapdoor and onto the staircase. Down, down, down into the darkness went Aladdin. He hurried through several gloomy caves and finally reached a beautiful garden. Many trees were growing there, covered in brightly coloured fruits. Aladdin couldn't resist picking handfuls of the glassy fruits and filling his pockets and shirt. He gasped with relief as he saw a rusty lamp resting on the grass, and he stuffed that into his shirt too. Then he was off back through the caves . . .

Now Aladdin hadn't spent all that time on the streets without becoming very streetwise. He was highly suspicious about his so-called uncle and, of course, Aladdin's suspicions were right. The merchant was in fact an evil sorcerer who knew powerful black magic. The sorcerer's wicked arts had shown him the whereabouts of the cave and the powers of the secret lamp that lay within, and he had worked for years to try to find a way in. Eventually, the sorcerer discovered that no one was allowed to enter the cave and take the lamp for themselves. Someone else had to do it for them – someone like a street-urchin, who wouldn't be missed. Because that someone had to remain locked in the cave forever!

Now Aladdin could see the sorcerer's eyes glinting greedily down through the square hole that led to the upper world. "Give me the lamp!" the sorcerer barked.

All Aladdin wanted to do was to get out of there as quickly as possible. "Help me out first and then I'll give it to you," he shouted back.

"I said, give me the lamp!" the sorcerer insisted.

Aladdin wasn't stupid. "Sure," he yelled, "just as soon as you get me out of here!"

"GIVE ME THE LAMP, YOU STUPID BOY!" roared the sorcerer.

Well, that did it. Aladdin hated people telling him he was worthless. "NO!" he shouted. "I found it and now I'm going to keep it!"

The sorcerer hopped about with rage, cursing and spluttering. "Then have it," he screamed, "and enjoy it in the darkness forever!" He thundered out the magic words and the trapdoor slammed shut with a massive crash. When Aladdin put his hands up and felt about, the opening was gone.

"What have I done!" Aladdin moaned, wringing his hands. As he did so, he happened to rub the sorcerer's ring. There was a blinding flash and a huge genie stood before him.

"I am the genie of the ring!" the massive apparition thundered. "Speak your wish, O master, and I will obey.

"I wish to heaven I was out of this cave!" Aladdin howled.

At once, Aladdin found himself back on the sands of the desert, blinking in the hot sunlight. He raced home and blurted out his whole sorry adventure to his mother. At first she thought he was telling one of his usual stories, but then Aladdin showed her the multi-coloured glass fruits and rusty old lamp.

"If we sell these glittery baubles and this old lamp," his mother sighed, "we'll at least have some pennies to buy some bread and cheese to go with our soup tonight."

"But we won't get the best price for the lamp unless I try to clean it up a bit," said Aladdin. He picked it up and began to rub at it with his sleeve.

Once more, there was a blinding flash and a genie even bigger than the genie of the ring stood before him. "I am the genie of the lamp!" roared the enormous spirit. "Speak your wish, O master, and I will obey."

"Bring us some food!" was the Aladdin's command.

Suddenly there was a table before them, covered with huge golden platters laden with delicious food. Aladdin and his mother could hardly believe their eyes. In a few minutes, their stomachs were more full than they had been in years. And after they'd sold one of the gold platters in the market, their purses were too.

After that, the lives of Aladdin and his mother

changed for the better. They were clever not to arouse suspicion by selling the gold platters only one at a time, when their purses were becoming empty. No one would have called them rich, although they lived much more comfortably than they had before. And so life would probably have gone on, if Aladdin hadn't been caught up in town one day in a great procession. Hundreds of slaves with swords at their sides came marching through the bazaar, and in the middle of them, high on their shoulders, was a magnificent litter of gold and silver. As the litter was carried past Aladdin, the swishing silk curtains swung just a little to one side, and inside Aladdin glimpsed the beautiful Princess Balroubadour.

From that moment on, Aladdin was head over heels in love. He couldn't speak, he couldn't eat, he couldn't sleep, for thinking of the beautiful

Princess Balroubadour. Aladdin's mother
watched her son grow thinner and paler by the
day, and finally decided she had to do something
about it – even if it was the most foolish thing
she had ever done in her life. She loaded up one
of the golden platters with the coloured, glassy
fruits that Aladdin had brought back from the
sorcerer's cave, and she went to see the princess's
father – the Sultan of Baghdad himself!

Of course, the sultan realized what the jewels
were at once – and he had never seen such huge,
fine diamonds, emeralds, rubies and sapphires in
his life. Being a greedy man, and hoping that
there were more where those came from, he
agreed at once that Aladdin should marry his
daughter and become his son-in-law.

Aladdin was overjoyed, and that night he
dared to use the lamp once more and conjure up
the genie. By morning, a splendid palace with

golden domes and pearl spires and nine hundred and ninety-nine stained glass windows had been built exactly opposite the sultan's own palace. The sultan clapped his hands with delight, the wedding festivities were held that very afternoon, and Aladdin took his beautiful bride to live in his splendid new home.

It was fortunate that Princess Balroubadour felt the same way about Aladdin as he felt about her, and together they were completely happy – until one day, when Aladdin was out hunting, a ragged old pedlar came through the streets of the bazaar shouting, "New lamps for old! New lamps for old!" The princess and her maid rushed to the eighty-eighth window of the palace to look out on the funny little man who was offering to swap good wares for bad.

How silly!" the maid giggled, and rushed to exchange the rusty old lamp in Aladdin's room. As soon as Aladdin's lamp was in the pedlar's hands, he gave a little cry of excitement and disappeared through the streets. A few seconds later, the princess, her maid and the entire palace had vanished, too! As you have probably guessed, the pedlar was none other than the wicked sorcerer.

Aladdin returned from his hunting trip to find his wife missing, his palace gone and his father-in-law furious! "Bring me my daughter within forty days," the Sultan roared, "or I'll stuff your precious jewels into your mouth and make you eat them!"

Worst of all, Aladdin no longer had his wonderful lamp. "What am I going to do?" he moaned, standing all alone in the spot where his palace had once been. He wrung his hands in despair, and as he did so, he rubbed the sorcerer's magic ring. In a flash, the genie of the ring stood before him once more. "Speak your wish, O master, and I will obey," boomed the mighty spirit.

"Bring back my palace, with everyone and everything in it!" yelped the delighted Aladdin.

But the genie shook his head firmly and said, "I cannot, master. The palace is under the power of the genie of the lamp."

Aladdin thought hard for a couple of seconds and then his face brightened. "Then take me to my wife!" he yelled.

Suddenly, Aladdin was standing in his palace in front of his startled – but overjoyed – wife. "Hurry," Princess Balroubadour urged. "The sorcerer is out at the moment, but he keeps the lamp with him at all times. We have to think of a way to get it from him."

The quickwitted Aladdin mixed a sleeping powder into a goblet of wine, gave it to the princess, and then hid behind a screen. Only a few moments later, the sorcerer came striding in, his cloak billowing out behind him. The smiling Princess Balroubadour rushed to offer him a refreshing drink – and as soon as the sorcerer had thirstily drained the sleeping potion, he collapsed on the floor in a crumpled heap.

Aladdin sprang out from behind the screen and fumbled in the sorcerer's clothes. At last, he held his lamp! He rubbed it, gave the order and in the twinkling of an eye, he, his wife, his palace – and the sorcerer – were back in Baghdad.

Aladdin and Princess Balroubadour breathed a sigh of relief. "I don't know about you," Aladdin said, "but I've had enough magic for one lifetime – and now I've got you, I've got everything I could possibly want." The princess nodded in agreement, and Aladdin once more rubbed his lamp. "I give you your freedom!" he told the genie, and in a flash the spirit was gone forever.

Aladdin and the Princess lived happily ever after. When the sorcerer eventually woke, he got what he had always wanted – the rusty old lamp, no more and no less.

Teddy Bear, Teddy Bear

Teddy bear, teddy bear, touch the ground.

Teddy bear, teddy bear, turn around.

Teddy bear, teddy bear, show your shoe

Teddy bear, teddy bear, that will do.

Teddy bear, teddy bear, run upstairs.

Teddy bear, teddy bear, say your prayers.

Teddy bear, teddy bear, blow out the light.

Teddy bear, teddy bear,

Say GOODNIGHT.

Hansel and Gretel

A retelling from the original tale by the Brothers Grimm

At the edge of a deep, dark forest there lived a poor woodcutter and his wife, a mean spiteful woman, and their two children Hansel and Gretel. The family was very poor and there was often very little food on the table.

One dreadful day there was no food at all and everyone went to bed hungry. Hansel could not sleep, and so it was that he heard his mother talking to his father. "Husband," she said in her thin spiteful voice, "there are too many mouths to feed. You must leave the children in the forest tomorrow."

"Wife, I cannot abandon our children, there are wolves in the forest!" said the poor woodcutter.

But his wife would give him no peace until he

had agreed to her wicked plan. Hansel felt his heart grow icy cold. But he was a clever boy and so he slipped out of the house and filled his pockets with the shiny white stones that lay scattered around the house.

The next morning they all rose early and Hansel and Gretel followed their father deep into the forest. He lit them a fire and told them he was

going to gather wood and would be back to collect them. He left them, tears falling down his face.

The day passed slowly. Hansel kept their fire going but when night fell, it grew very cold and they could hear all kinds of rustling under the shadowy trees. Gretel could not understand why their father had not come back to collect them, so Hansel had to tell her that their mother had told the woodcutter to leave them there deliberately.

"Don't worry, Gretel," he said, "I will lead us back home," and there, clear in the moonlight, he showed her the line of white stones that he had dropped from his pocket one by one that morning as their father had led them into the forest. They were soon home where there father greeted them with joy. But their mother was not pleased.

Some time passed. They managed to survive with little to eat but the day came when Hansel heard his mother tell the woodcutter to leave them in the forest again. This time when Hansel went to collect some more pebbles, he found his mother had locked the door and he couldn't get out.

In the morning, their father gave them a small piece of bread, and then led them even deeper into the forest than before. Hansel comforted Gretel and told her that this time he had left a trail of

breadcrumbs to lead them home. But when the
moon rose and the children set off there was not a
breadcrumb to be seen. The birds had eaten them.
There was nothing to do but sleep under a tree and
wait to see what they might do in the morning.

All next day they walked and walked, but they
saw nothing but trees. And the next day was the
same. By this time they were not only cold and
hungry but frightened, too. It seemed they would
never find a way out of the forest. But just as it was
getting dark, they came to a
clearing and there stood a
strange house.

The walls were
made of
gingerbread, the
windows of fine
spun sugar and
the tiles on the
roof were

brightly striped sweets. Hansel and Gretel could not believe their good luck and they were soon breaking off little bits of the amazing house to eat. But then a little voice came from inside.

"Nibble, nibble, little mouse,

Who is that eating my sweet house?"

Out of the front door came a very old woman. She smiled very sweetly at the children and said, "Dear children, you don't need to eat my house. Come inside and I will give you plenty to eat and you shall sleep in warm cosy beds tonight." Hansel and Gretel needed no second asking. They were soon tucked up, warm and full of hot milk and ginger biscuits and apples. They both fell asleep very quickly. But little did they know they were in worse danger than ever before. The old woman was a wicked witch and she had decided to make Gretel work in the kitchen, and worst of all, she planned to fatten Hansel up so she might eat him!

The next morning she locked Hansel in a cage

and gave Gretel a broom and told her to clean the gingerbread house from top to toe. In the evening, the witch fed Hansel a huge plate of chicken but she only gave poor Gretel a dry hunk of bread. But once she was asleep, Hansel shared his meal with Gretel. And so they lived for many days. The witch could not see very well. So every morning, the witch would make Hansel put his finger through the cage so she could tell how fat he was getting. But Hansel poked a chicken bone through the bars so she thought he was still too skinny to eat.

After many days, she grew fed up and decided to eat him anyway, and so she asked Gretel to help her prepare the big oven. The witch made some bread to go with her supper and when the oven was really hot she put it in to cook. The kitchen was soon filled with the lovely smell of baking bread, and the witch asked Gretel to lift the bread out to cool. But Gretel was clever too. She pretended she couldn't reach the tray, and when the witch bent down inside the oven Gretel gave her a great shove and closed the door with a clang. And that was the end of the witch!

Gretel released Hansel, and together they set off once more to try to find their way home. After all their adventures, fortune finally smiled on them and they soon found the path home where they were reunited with their father who was simply overjoyed to see them again. And what, you might ask, of their mean mother? Well, the poor woodcutter had not had a happy moment since he left the children in the forest. He had become so miserable that she decided there was no living with him. The day before Hansel and Gretel returned, she had upped sticks and left, so that served her right, didn't it?

Teeny-tiny

An English folk tale

Once upon a time there lived a teeny-tiny old woman. She lived in a teeny-tiny house in a teeny-tiny street with a teeny-tiny cat. One day the teeny-tiny woman decided to go out for a teeny-tiny walk. She put on her teeny-tiny boots and her teeny-tiny bonnet, and off she set.

When she had walked a teeny-tiny way down the teeny-tiny street, she went through a teeny-tiny gate into a teeny-tiny graveyard, which was a teeny-tiny shortcut to the teeny-tiny meadow. Well, she had only taken a few teeny-tiny steps when she saw a teeny-tiny bone lying on top of a teeny-tiny grave. She thought that would do very well to make some teeny-tiny soup for supper so she put the  teeny-tiny bone in her teeny-tiny pocket and went home at once to her teeny-tiny house.

Now the teeny-tiny woman was tired when she reached her teeny-tiny house so she did not make the teeny-tiny soup immediately but put the teeny-tiny bone into her teeny-tiny cupboard. Then she sat in her teeny-tiny chair and put her teeny-tiny feet up and had a teeny-tiny sleep. But she had only been asleep a teeny-tiny time when she woke up at the sound of a teeny-tiny voice coming from her teeny-tiny cupboard. The teeny-tiny voice said, "Where is my teeny-tiny bone?"

Well, the teeny-tiny woman was a teeny-tiny bit frightened so she wrapped her teeny-tiny shawl round her teeny-tiny head and went to sleep again. She had only been asleep a teeny-tiny time when the teeny-tiny voice came from the teeny-tiny cupboard again, a teeny-tiny bit louder this time. "Where is my teeny-tiny bone?"

The teeny-tiny woman was a teeny-tiny bit more frightened than last time so she hid under the teeny-tiny cushions, but she could not go back to sleep, not even a teeny-tiny bit. Then the teeny-tiny voice came again and this time it was even a teeny-tiny bit louder.

"Where is my teeny-tiny bone?"

This time the teeny-tiny woman sat up in her teeny-tiny chair and said in her loudest teeny-tiny voice, "TAKE IT!"

There was a teeny-tiny silence, and then a teeny-tiny ghost ran out of the teeny-tiny house, down the teeny-tiny street, through the teeny-tiny gate into the teeny-tiny graveyard – with the teeny-tiny bone clutched very tightly in its teeny-tiny hand! And the teeny-tiny woman never took even a teeny-tiny walk there ever again!

Acknowledgements

The publishers would like to thank the following
artists whose work appears in this book

June Allan
Julie Banyard
Rosalind Beardshaw
Candice Bekir
Jo Brown
George Buchanon
Vanessa Card
Denise Coble
Frank Endersby
Sally Holmes
Milena Jahier
Cecilia Johansson
Stephen Lambert
Priscilla Lamont
Mary Lonsdale
Vanessa Lubach
Diana Mayo
Debbie Meekcoms
A. Montgomery-Higham
Richard Morgan
Tracy Morgan
Tricia Newell
Elizabeth Sawyer
Susan Scott
Caroline Sharpe
Pam Smy
Gwen Tourret
Peter Utton
Mike Walsh